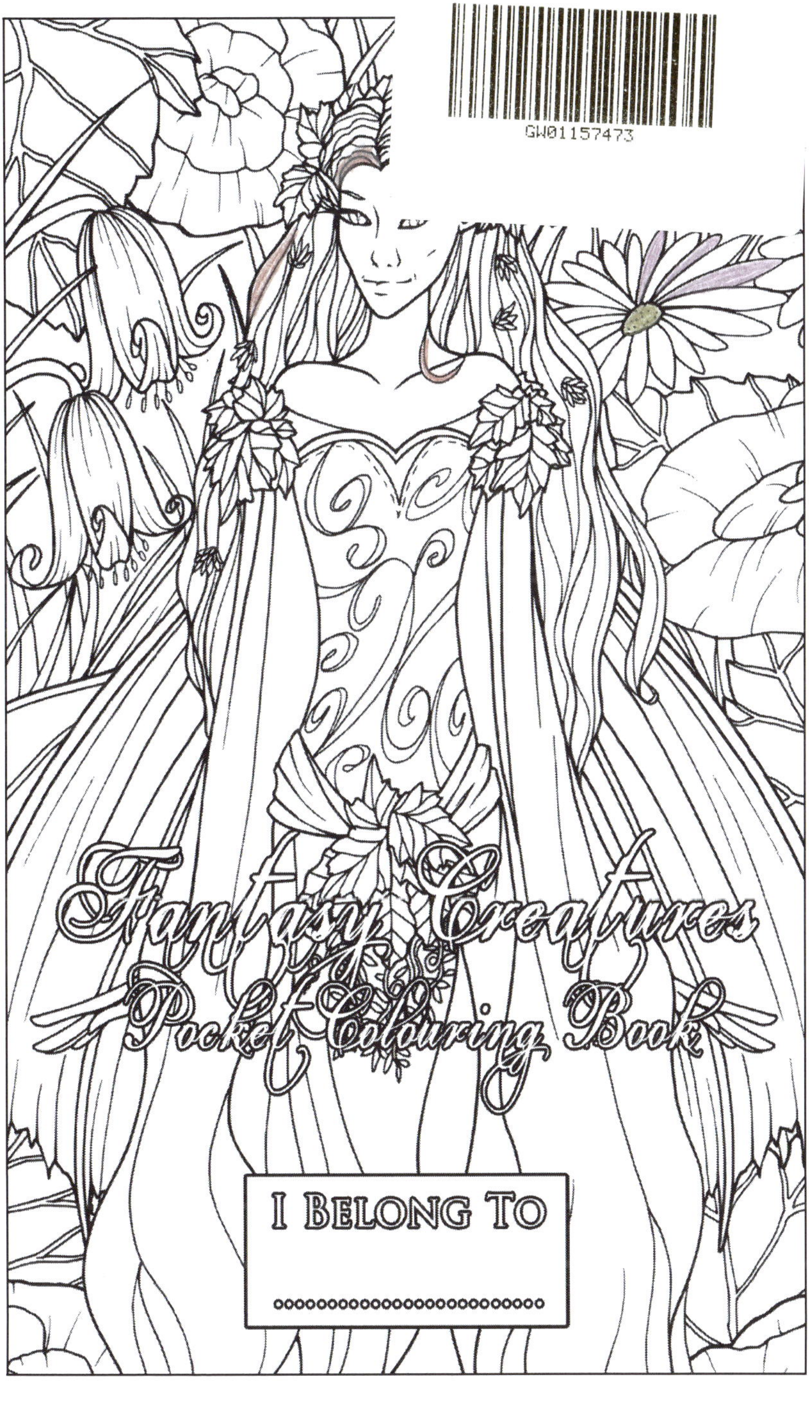
Fantasy Creatures
Pocket Colouring Book
I Belong To
....

Colouring Books For Grownups series

The Wild Colouring Book
The Calm Colouring Book
The Exotic Colouring Book
The Bumper Colouring Book
Fantasy Creatures Colouring Book

Miniature colouring books

Fantasy Creatures Pocket Colouring Book

Colouring Books For Grownups Companion Books

2016/17 diaries
(day per page, week per page & week per view)
[Available/coming soon for the Wild, Calm, Exotic & Fantasy Colouring Books]

A4 notebooks
[Available for the Wild, Calm, Exotic & Fantasy Colouring Books]

A5 notebooks
[Available for the Wild, Calm, Exotic & Fantasy Colouring Books]

Published in 2016 by
Createspace Publishing
4900 LaCross Road
North Charleston, SC 29406
USA

© Meg Cowley 2016

The moral rights of the author have been asserted.

All rights reserved. No part of this publication may be reproduced, stored, copied or shared by any means, electronic or physical, or used in any manner without the prior written consent of the illustrator. The artist grants permission for the owner of this title to photocopy pages for their personal use only. Redistribution or sharing of blank pages is prohibited.

ISBN: 978-1532932687

Created by Meg Cowley
www.megcowley.com

Welcome to the

Fantasy Creatures Pocket Colouring Book

This book contains twenty-five original, hand-drawn illustrations, featuring fantastical fantasy subjects. Discover fantasy creatures old and new across these pages, and learn about them in the Fantasy Creature Bestiary overleaf.

Each drawing is replicated, giving two copies of each drawing to colour in; enjoy keeping a blank copy, using two colour schemes or even gifting one of your finished, coloured pages to a friend!

Colouring is just one way of expressing creativity. This book is perfect for those who prefer colouring to designing – you can bring my art to life! When inspiration strikes, add in your own doodles and designs in the spaces.

Being creative is a great way to relieve stress. It's important to take a step back from our hectic lives to ensure we stay happy and healthy, both mentally and physically. It's also a great way to step out of our digital world for a while and enjoy a hands on activity.

The designs range in complexity, so you can find one that matches your mood – a quick colouring blast, or an afternoon snuggled up with your colouring tools.

The Fantasy Creatures Pocket Colouring Book is designed practically to make it easy to colour. The designs don't go into the spine or to the page edge, so every inch is accessible. There's also one design per double page – so feel free to use felt tips. You won't have to worry about damaging a drawing on the reverse side.

In addition, this makes it easy if you want to cut a design out to frame it – feel free! Art should be enjoyed after you've created it too.

Last of all…

Happy Colouring!

Fantasy Creature Bestiary

Centaur

A fantastical creature with the lower body and legs of a horse, and the head, arms and torso of a human, originating from Greek mythology and spreading through many other later cultures across the globe. Centaurs are depicted throughout history as chariot pullers and fighters.

Dragon

A legendary creature featuring in the myths and tales of many cultures across the world. Dragons are typically depicted with serpentine and reptilian properties, such as scales. Depending on the subspecies of dragon, they may have rear limbs, forelimbs, be limbless, and have wings, or be flightless. Depicted in this title is the great dragon; a winged beast with four limbs. In some tales, dragons are fire breathers.

Dryad

A type of nymph; dryads are tree nymphs, supernatural beings who are tied to their home tree. These tree spirits are extremely shy, so they are rare to behold.

Elf

A supernatural, magical and in some cases immortal being of extreme beauty reported in Old English and Norse mythology. Elvish nature varies widely across cultures; some helping humans, some ambivalent towards them, and some hindering or harming them.

Faerie (also known as fairy, fey folk)

A supernatural, magical and enchanting being or spirit from European folklore. Faeries are human in appearance, although historically 'fairy' was used to refer also to goblins or gnomes, and diminutive in size. It is mainly in post-Victorian tales and artwork that faeries are depicted with wings.

Faerie Circle (also known as a fairy ring)

A faerie circle, also called a fairy ring, or elf circle/ring, is explained in modern times as a naturally occurring ring or arc of mushrooms. In fantasy culture, a faerie ring however, is a perilous place for mortals to step. They are said to be the result of fairies dancing. Mortals who step within a faerie ring may perceive the faeries, but may also become trapped within the ring and fall under the faeries' spell, never to escape.

Faun

A creature of with the upper half of a human, lower half of a goat and horns of a goat. Fauns are spirits of the forest, as mischievous and unreliable as many of their companions, who can help or hinder humans at will.

Goblin

A malevolent and greedy creature, linked in folklore to devils and demons. Traditionally depicted as small creatures, related to brownies and gnomes, goblins are also sometimes ascribed magical abilities.

Grim (also known as gwyllgi, gytrash, dog of darkness, black dog, or barghest)

A malevolent beast of nightmares primarily found in British folklore. Given various names, the grim is described as a black dog, wolf or canine of terrifying proportion, with large, glowing eyes. Grims are associated with death.

Gryphon (also known as a griffin)

A legendary creature with the head, wings and forelegs of an eagle, and body and hindquarters of a lion. Gryphons are considered to be powerful and majestic creatures, associated with guarding treasures and possessions of priceless value.

Hippogriff (also known as a hippogryff)

A legendary creature originating in Greek mythology with the head, wings and forelegs of a gryphon, and the body and hindquarters of a horse.

Imp

Imps are small creatures similar to goblins and associated with demons and familiars/companions of witches. Unlike goblins, imps are not considered evil creatures, but they are extremely mischievous and untamable.

King of the Forest

A stag; the grandest creature of the forest. In mythology, deer are associated with woodland deities, and white stags feature in many folk tales.

Knucker

A water dragon or water monster featuring in various tales and myths. In Norse mythology, Jörmungandr was a water dragon so huge he was able to encircle the earth and grasp his own tail.

Kraken

A legendary sea creature of gigantic proportion. In modern culture, krakens are mostly described as, and associated with, giant squid or octopus, though early tales describe them more akin to a giant whale or crab.

Mermaid

An aquatic dwelling creature with the tail of a fish, and the head and upper body of a woman. Tales of mermaids occur around the globe; the oldest accounts are thousands of years old, and modern sightings are still reported. Their male counterparts are called mermen. Mermaids have been reported as both benevolent and malevolent in their actions towards humans, in particular sailors.

Phoenix

A bird of extremely long or infinite life, commonly associated with fire, for it regenerates and is reborn by rising from the ashes of its predecessor. Phoenixes are generally thought to be colourful birds, and there are many different colours of phoenix recorded.

Revenant

A once living creature returned from the grave to terrorize the living, in the form of a ghost or animated corpse. Common in medieval folklore, with counterparts in other cultures. Modern zombies share similarities with revenants, who are also linked to vampires as in some cultures, revenants were blood drinkers. In some accounts, revenants also have magical abilities.

Rune stone (or standing stone)

A large, upright, standing stone, found alone or in groups. Some have religious significance, but their true purposes are unknown. Some are used in burials as gravestones; rune stones are standing stones with inscriptions. Using the Anglo-Saxon rune chart below, can you decode the message on the rune stone colouring page?

A B C D E F G H I J K L M N
O P Q R S T U V W X Y Z EE

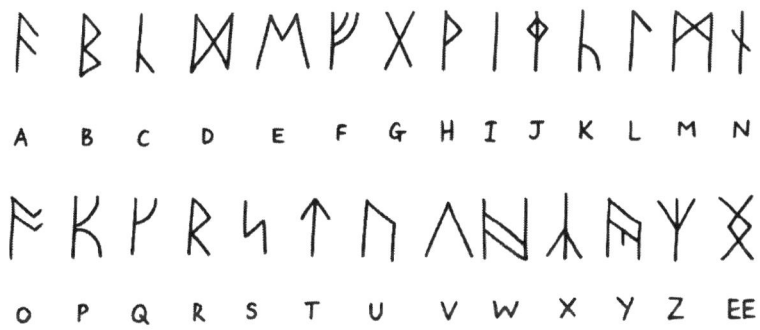

Siren

A creature of Greek mythology, sometimes associated with the mermaid. Sirens are traditionally depicted as beautiful humanoid creatures who lured sailors to their deaths with their enchanting music and singing.

Witch & Sorcerer (also known as an enchanter, wizard, or mage)

A man and woman who practice magic. Witches and sorcerers differ slightly; witches traditionally do not need physical tools or actions to curse or perform magic.

Wyvern

A legendary reptilian creature related to the dragon. A wyvern typically has a dragon's head, a scaled body and tail, hind legs and wings in place of forelimbs. That it only has two hind limbs and no forelimbs is what distinguishes it from a true dragon.

Unicorn

A fantasy beast appearing as a horse with a large, pointed, spiralling horn protruding from its forehead. A unicorn is a symbol of purity and is said to have healing powers.

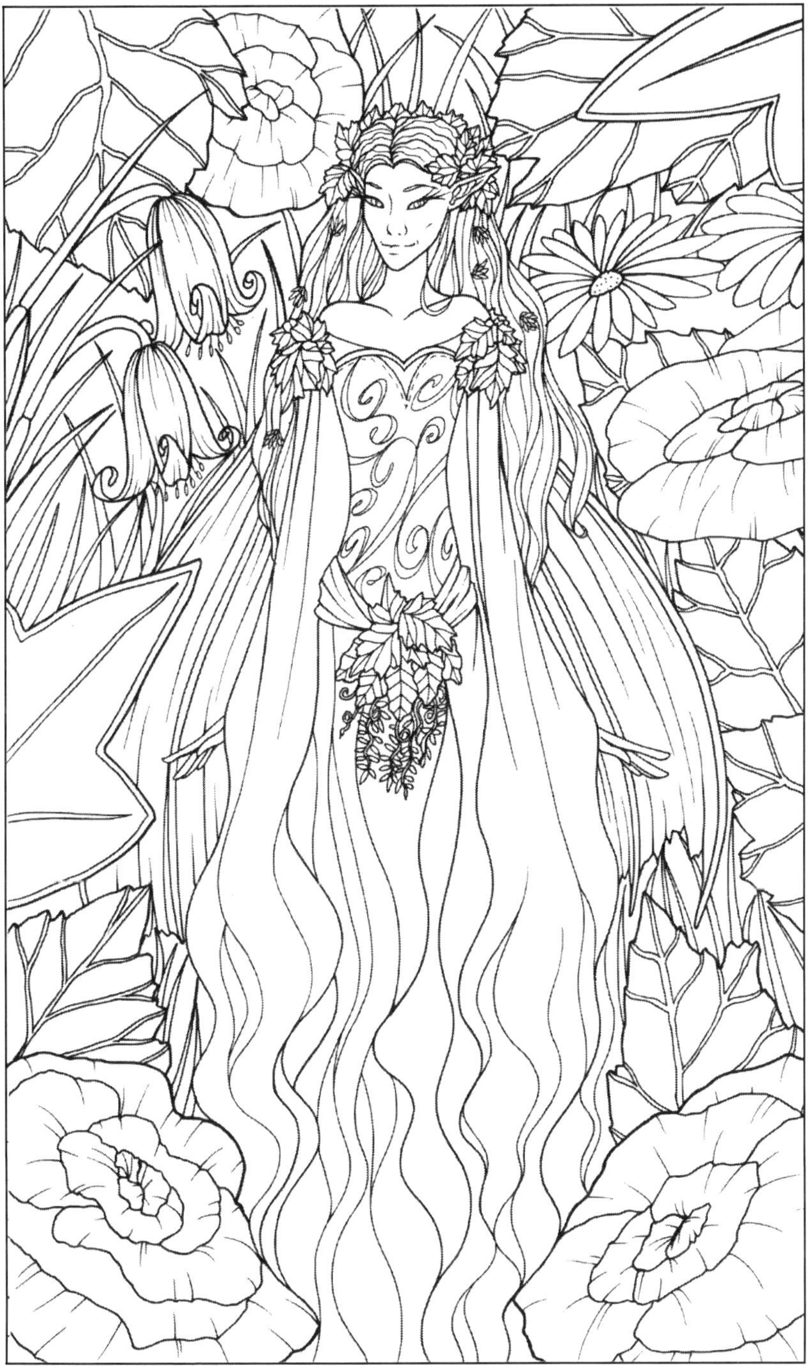

Faerie Queen

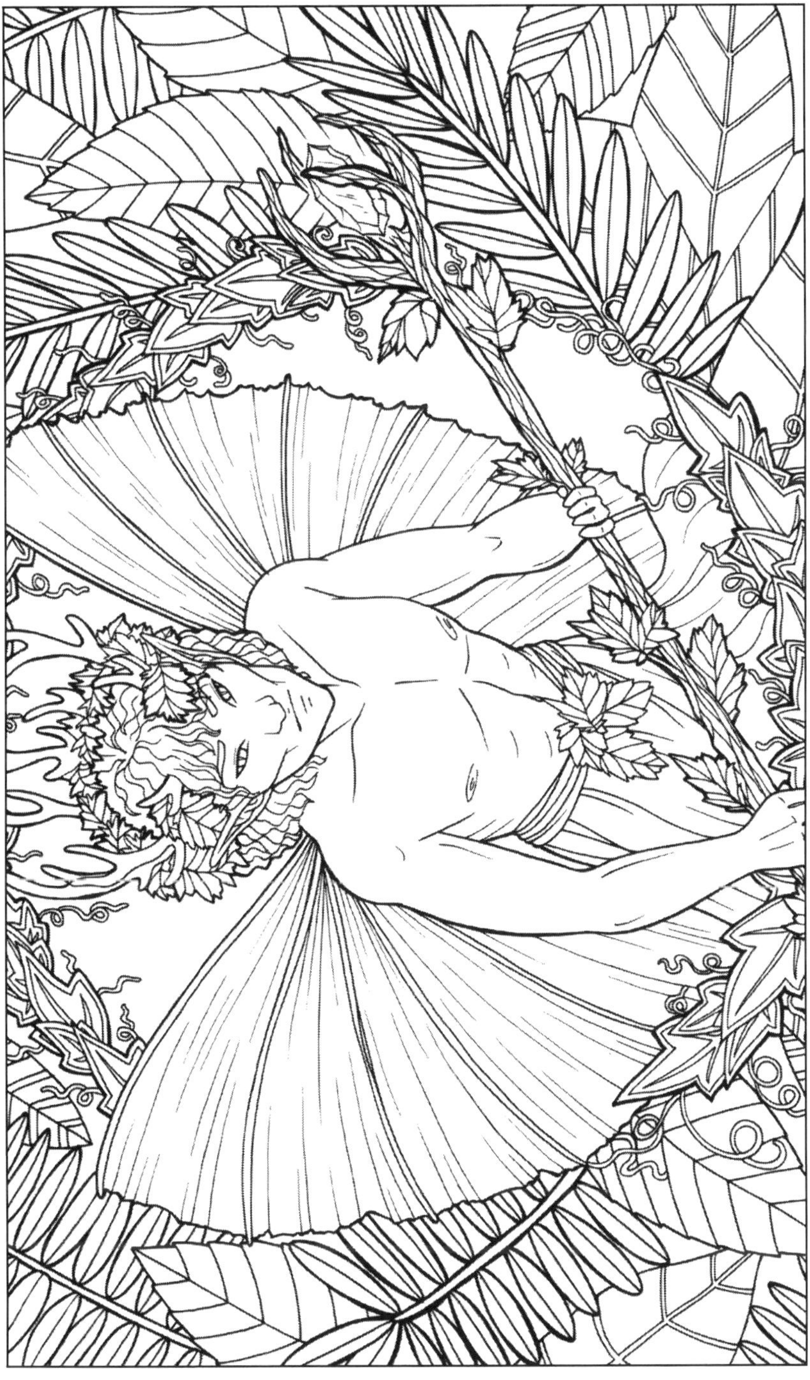

Faerie King

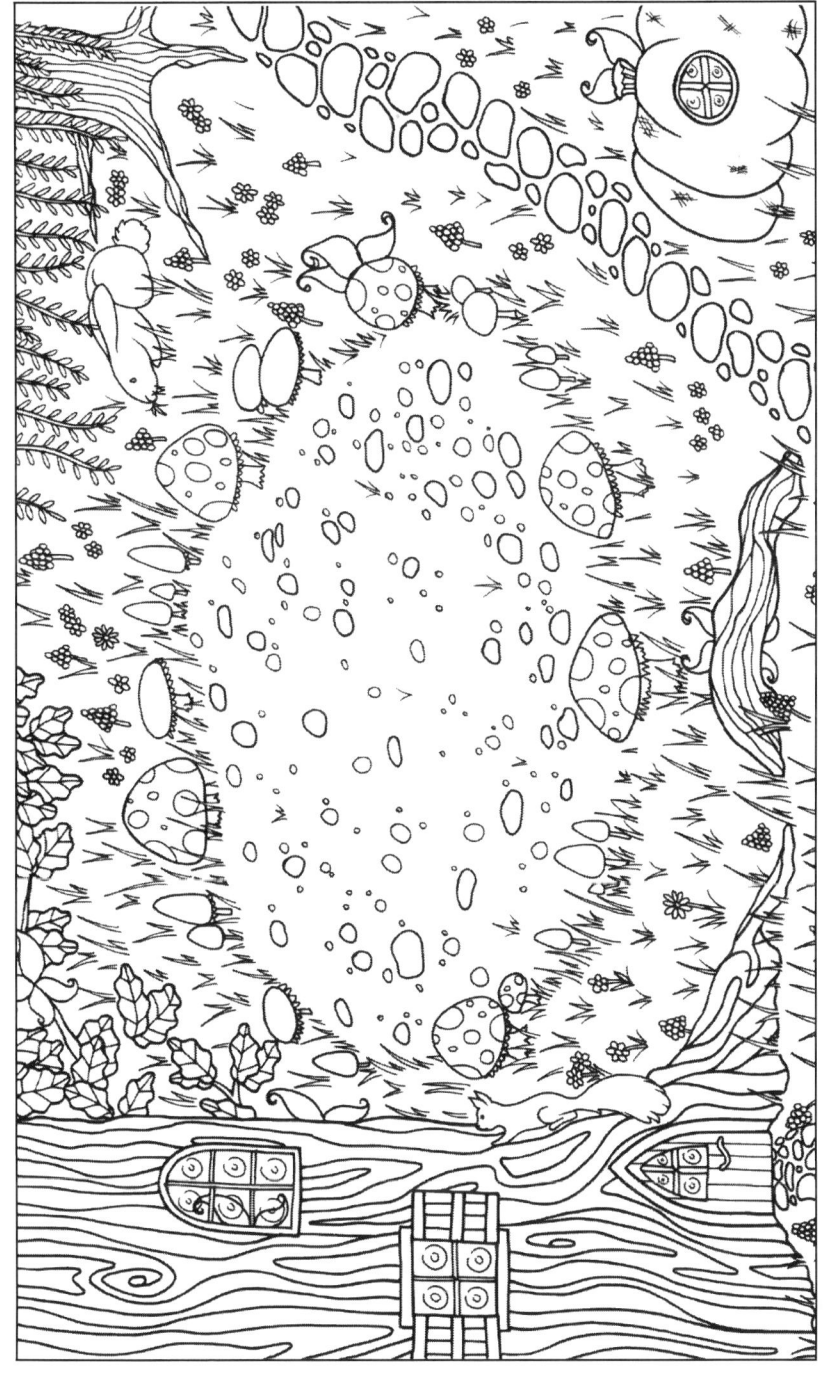

Faerie Circle

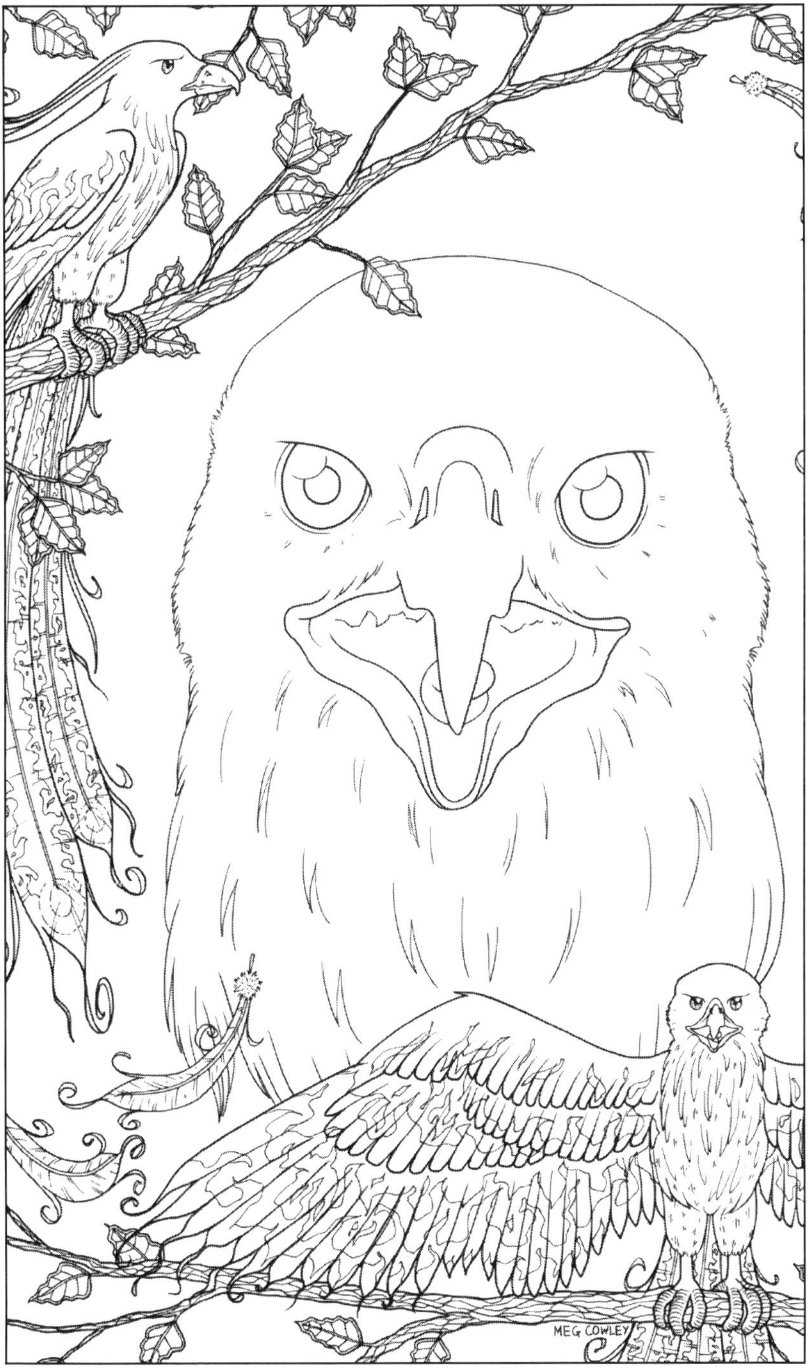
MEG COWLEY

Phoenix

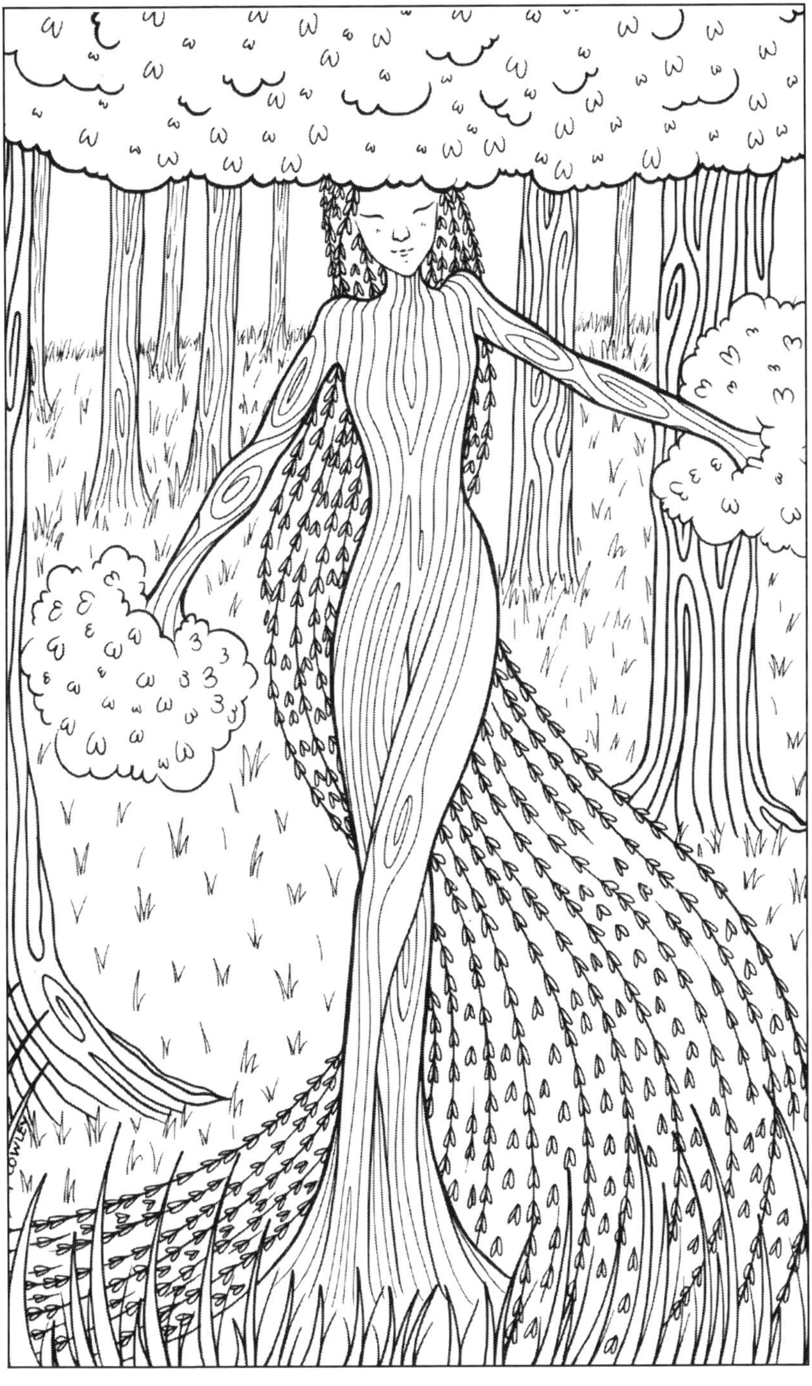

Dryad

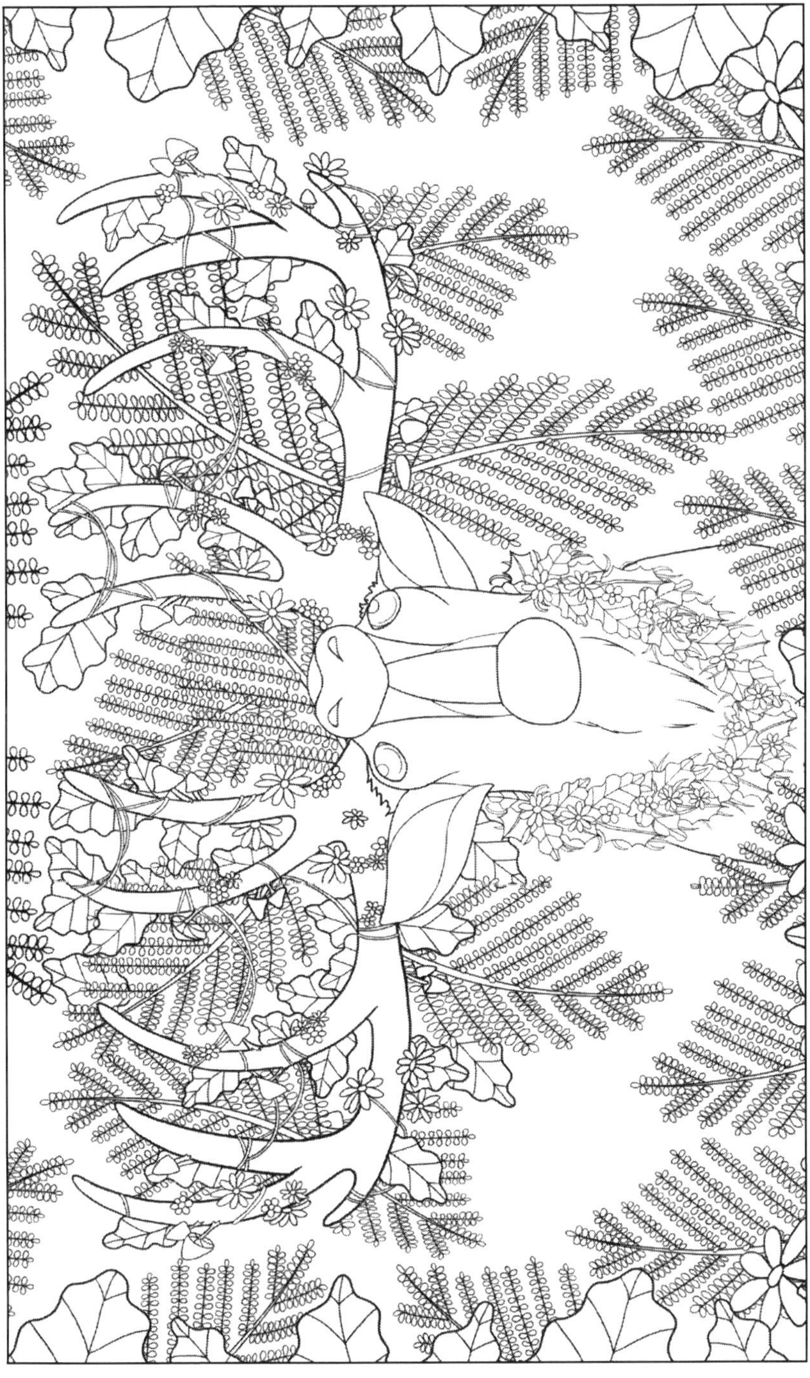

King of the Forest

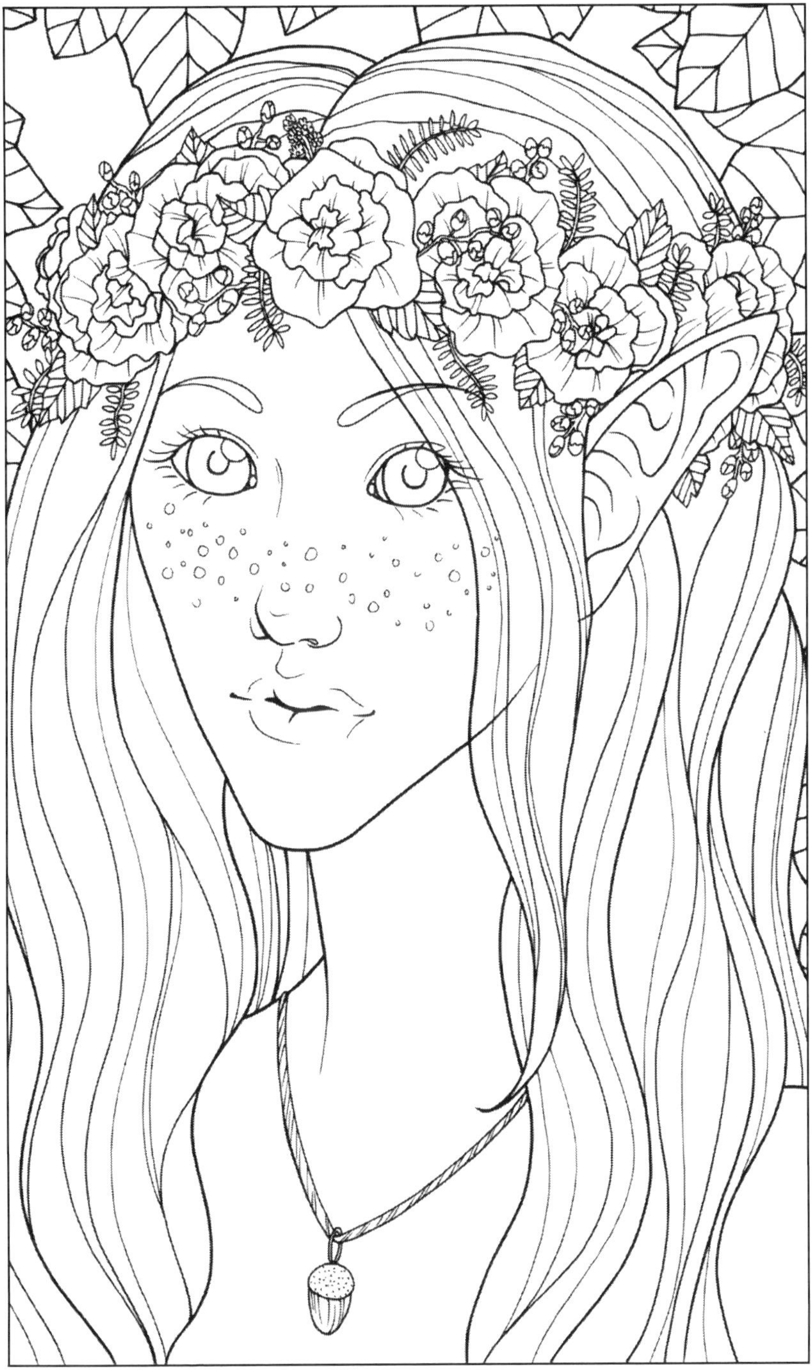

Elf

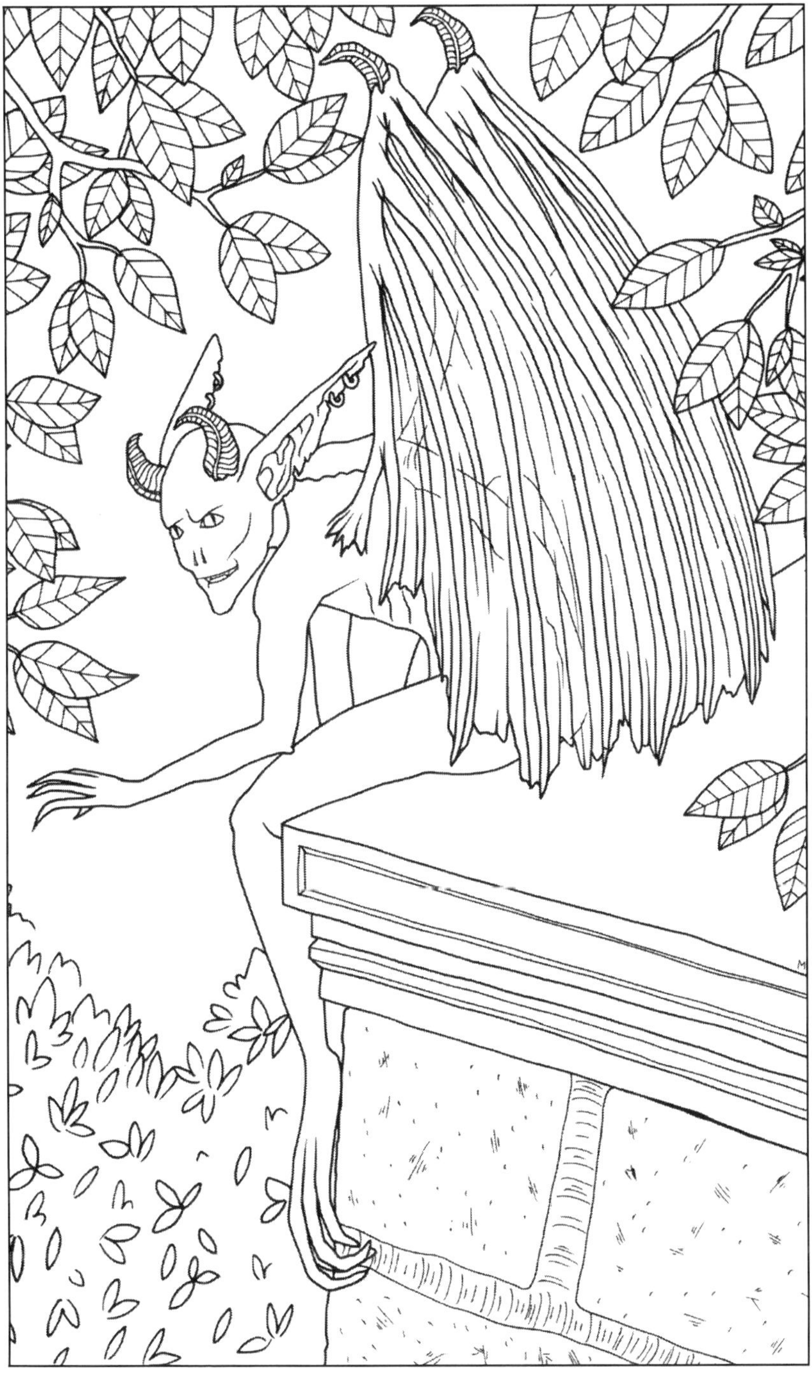

Imp

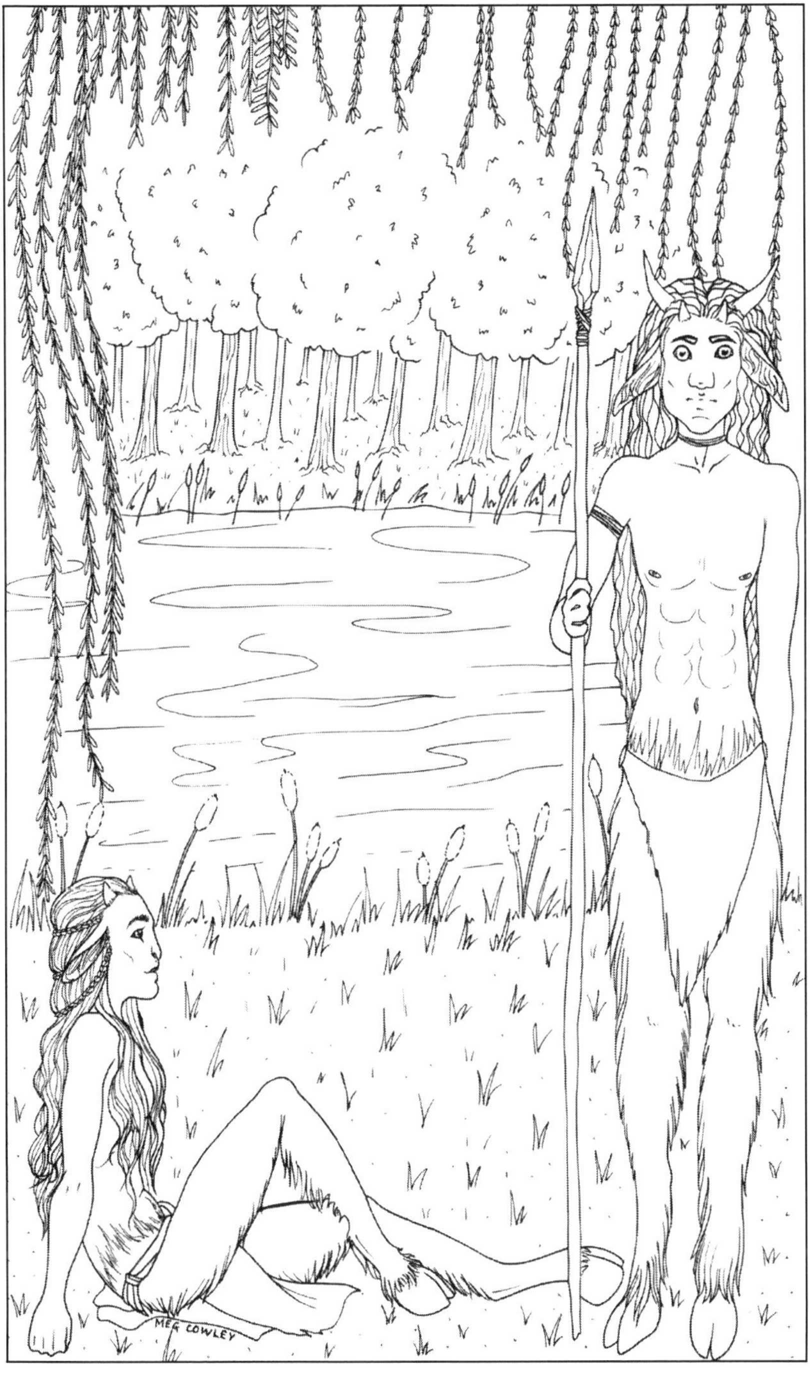
MEG COWLEY

Faun

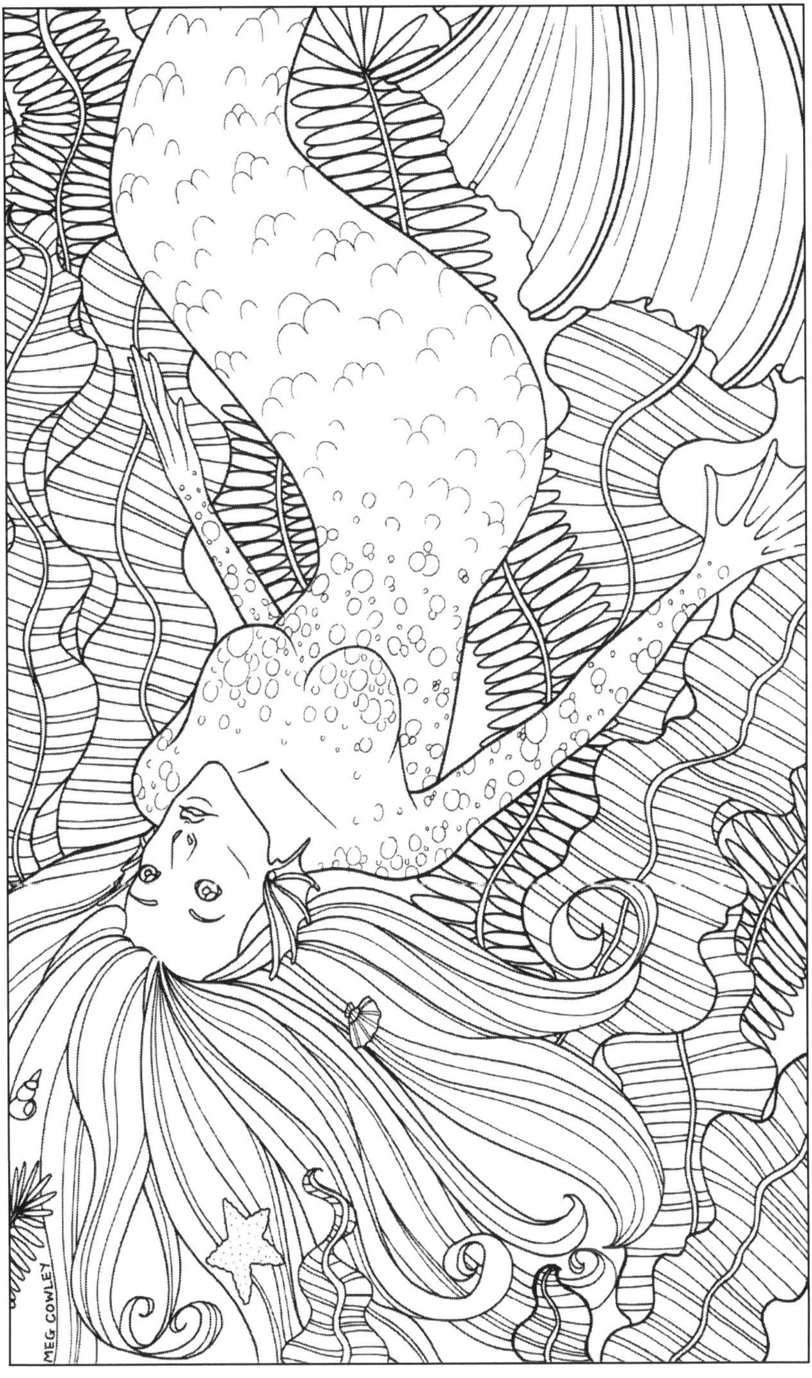
MEG COWLEY

Mermaid

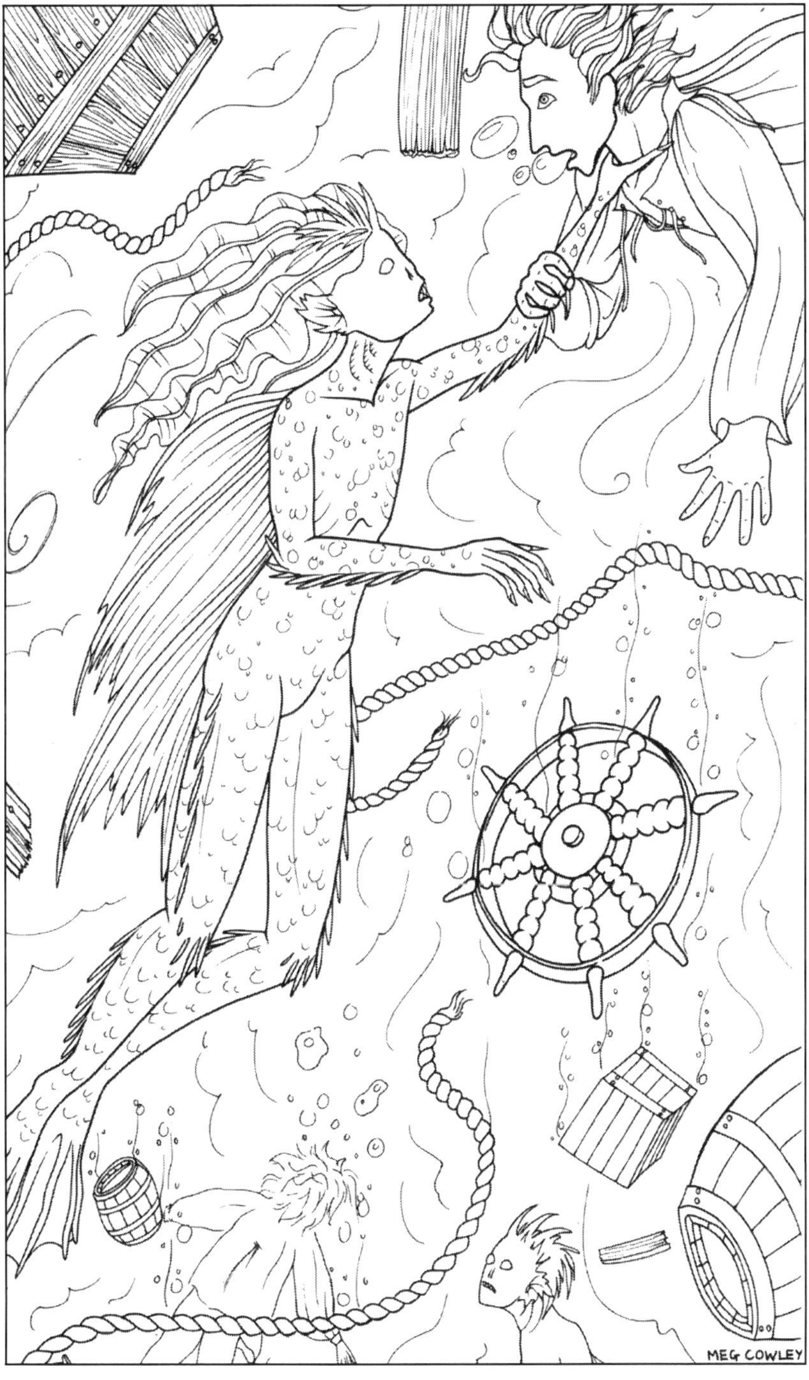
MEG COWLEY

Siren

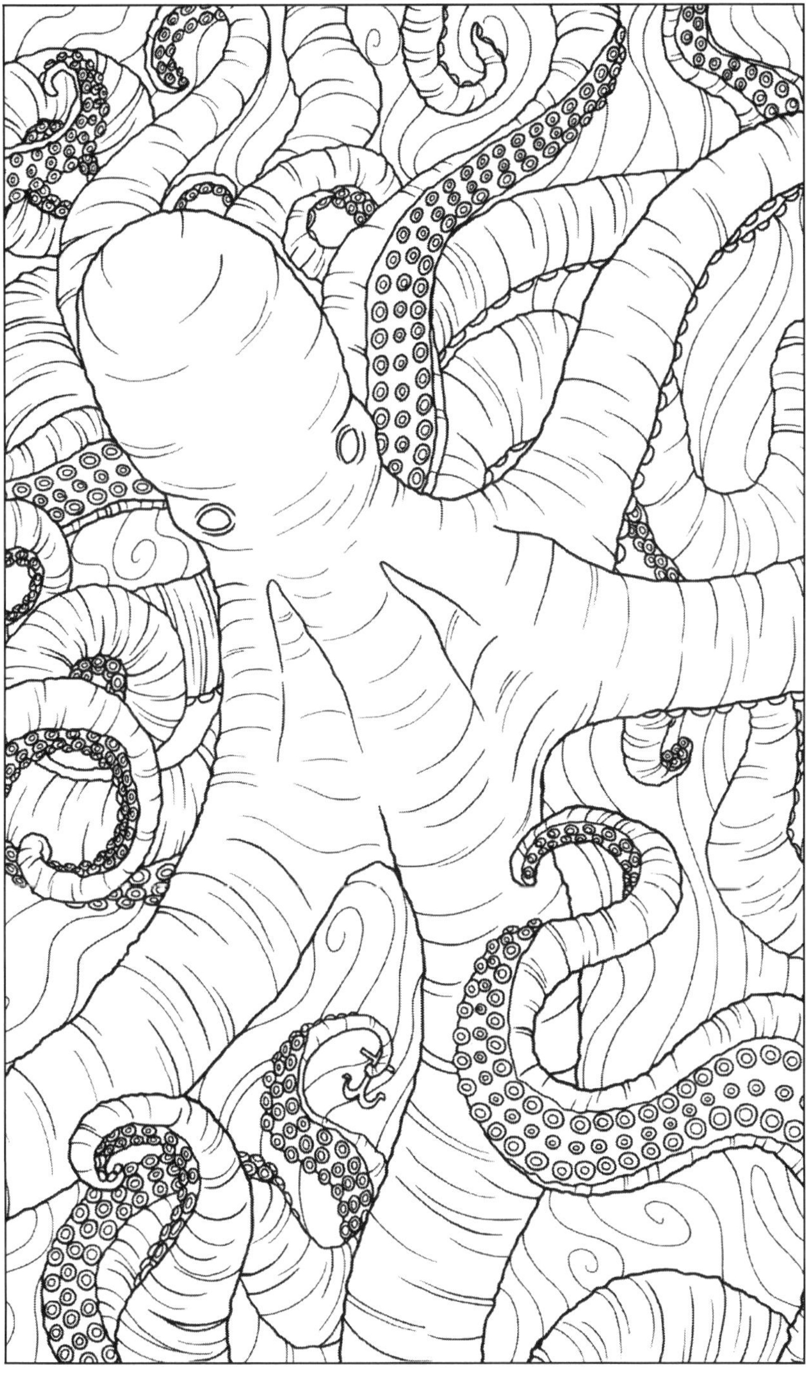

Kraken

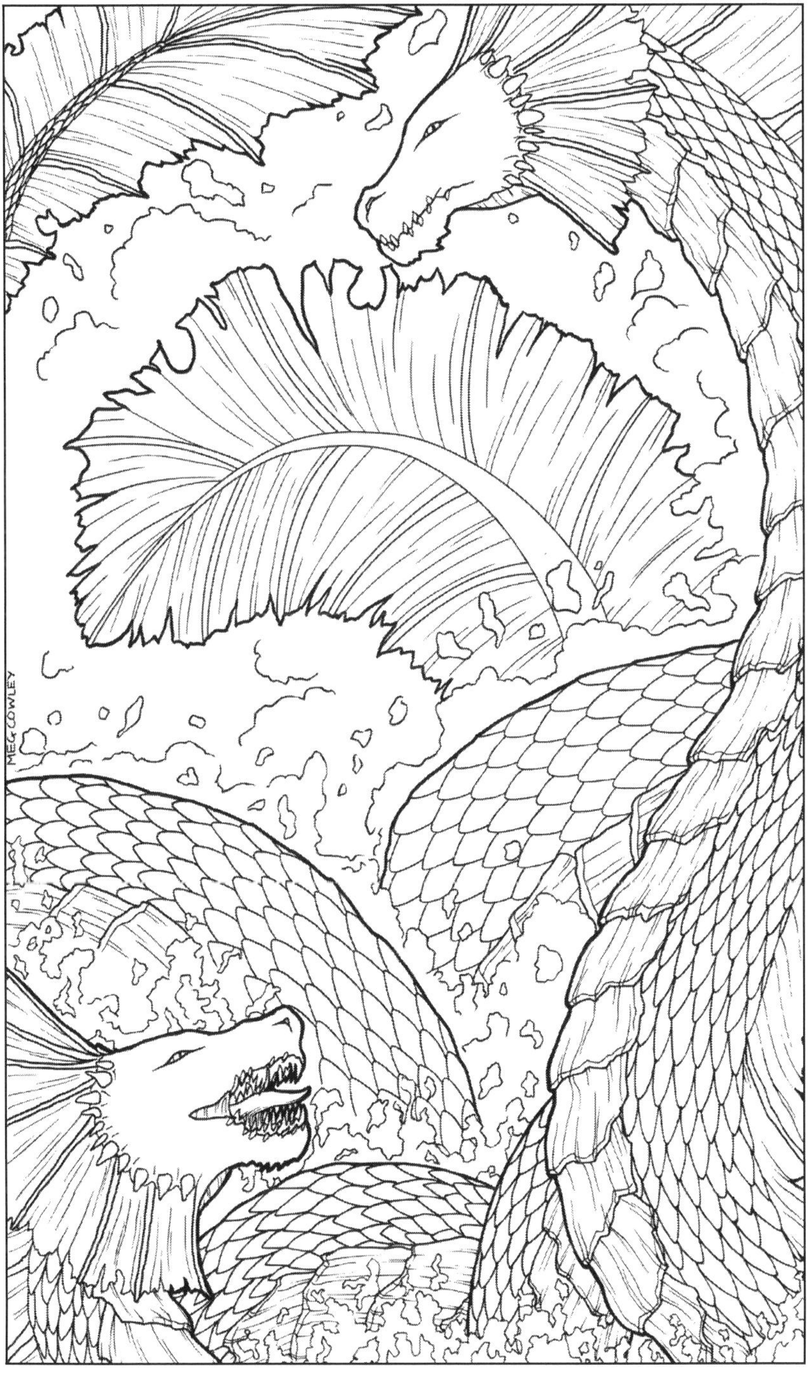
MEG COWLEY

Knucker

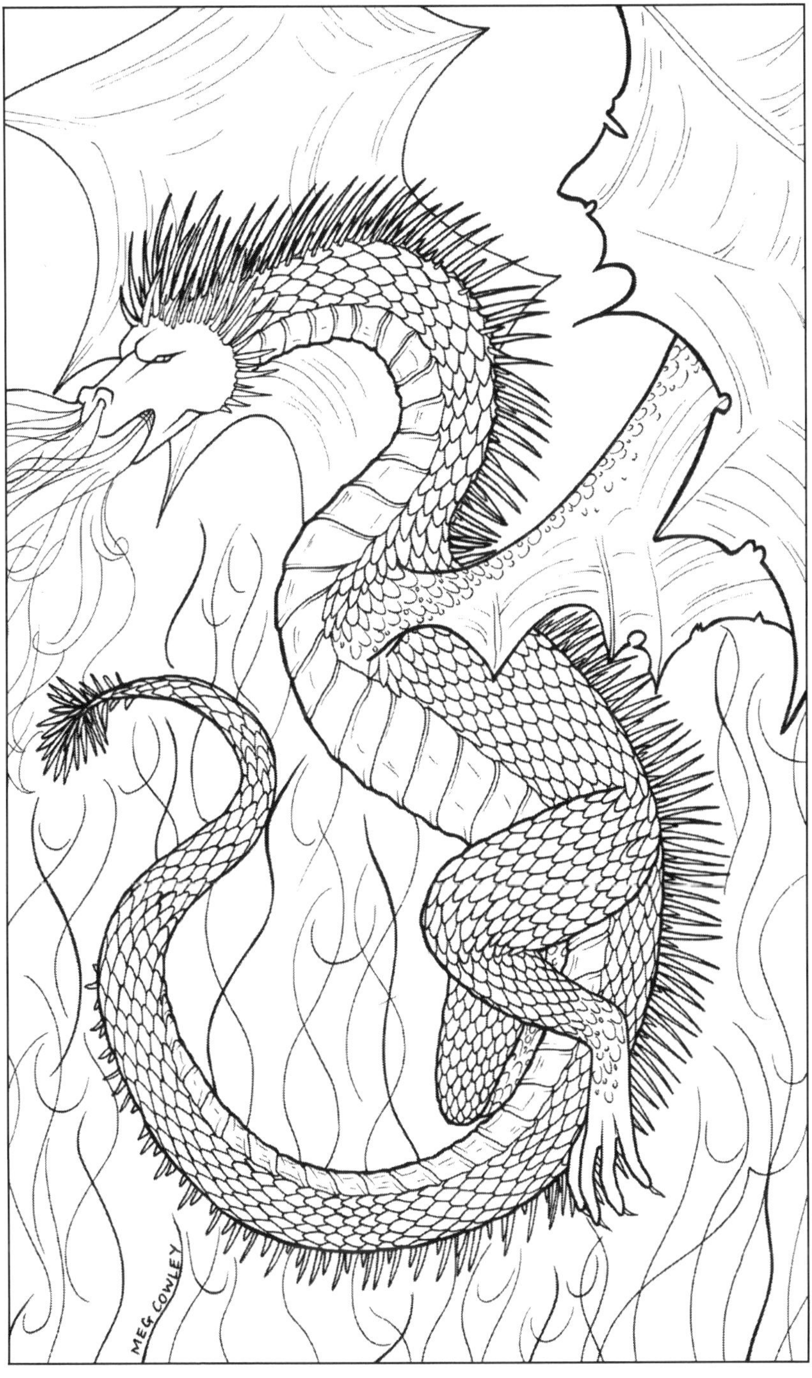
MEG COWLEY

Wyvern

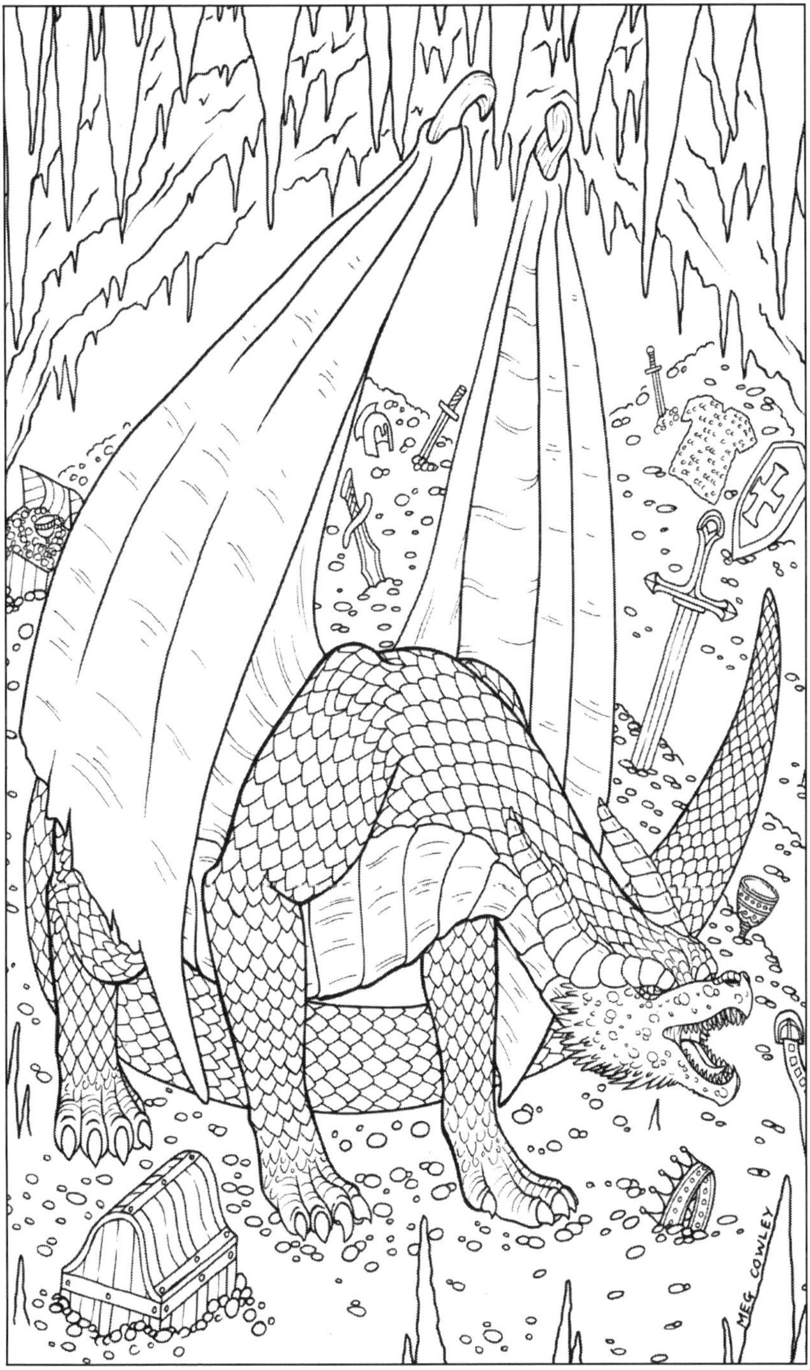
MEG COWLEY

Dragon

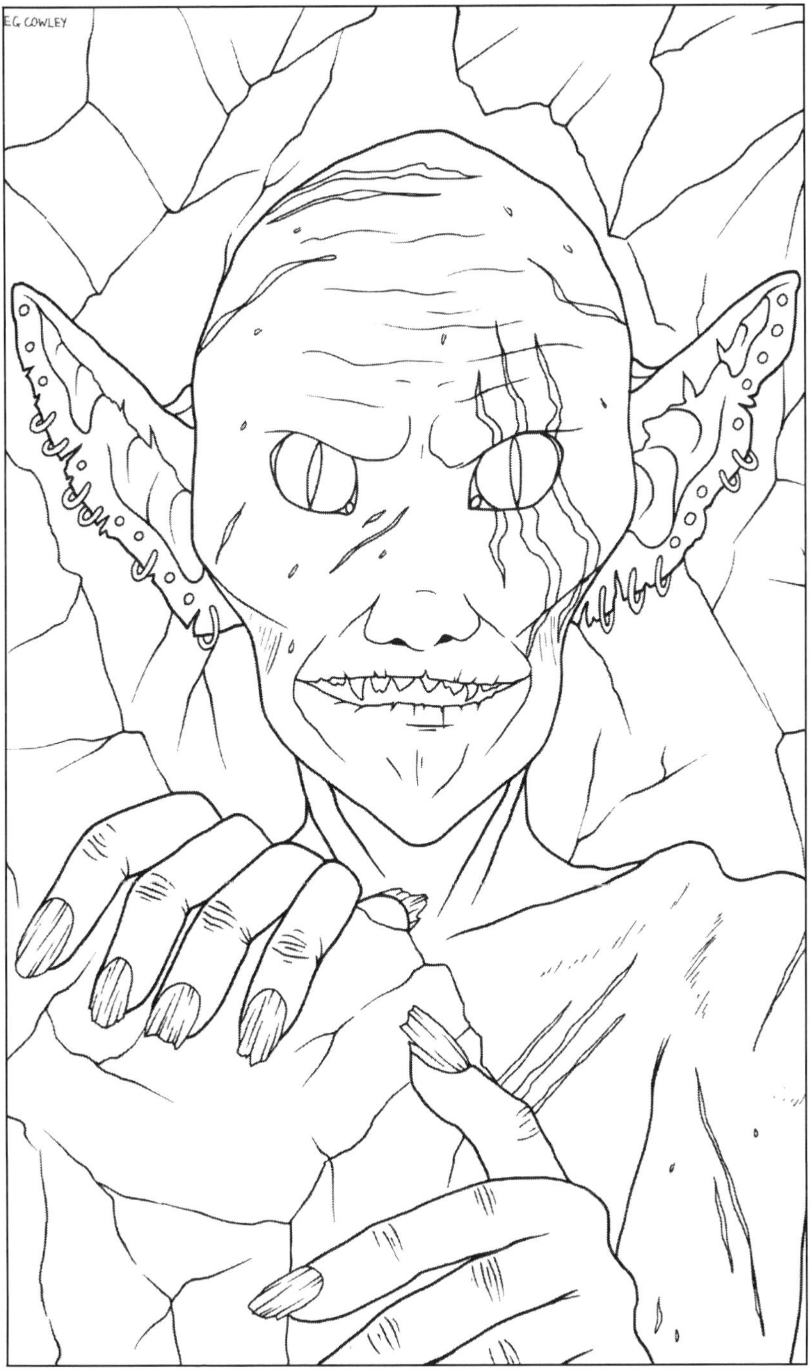
E.G. COWLEY

Goblin

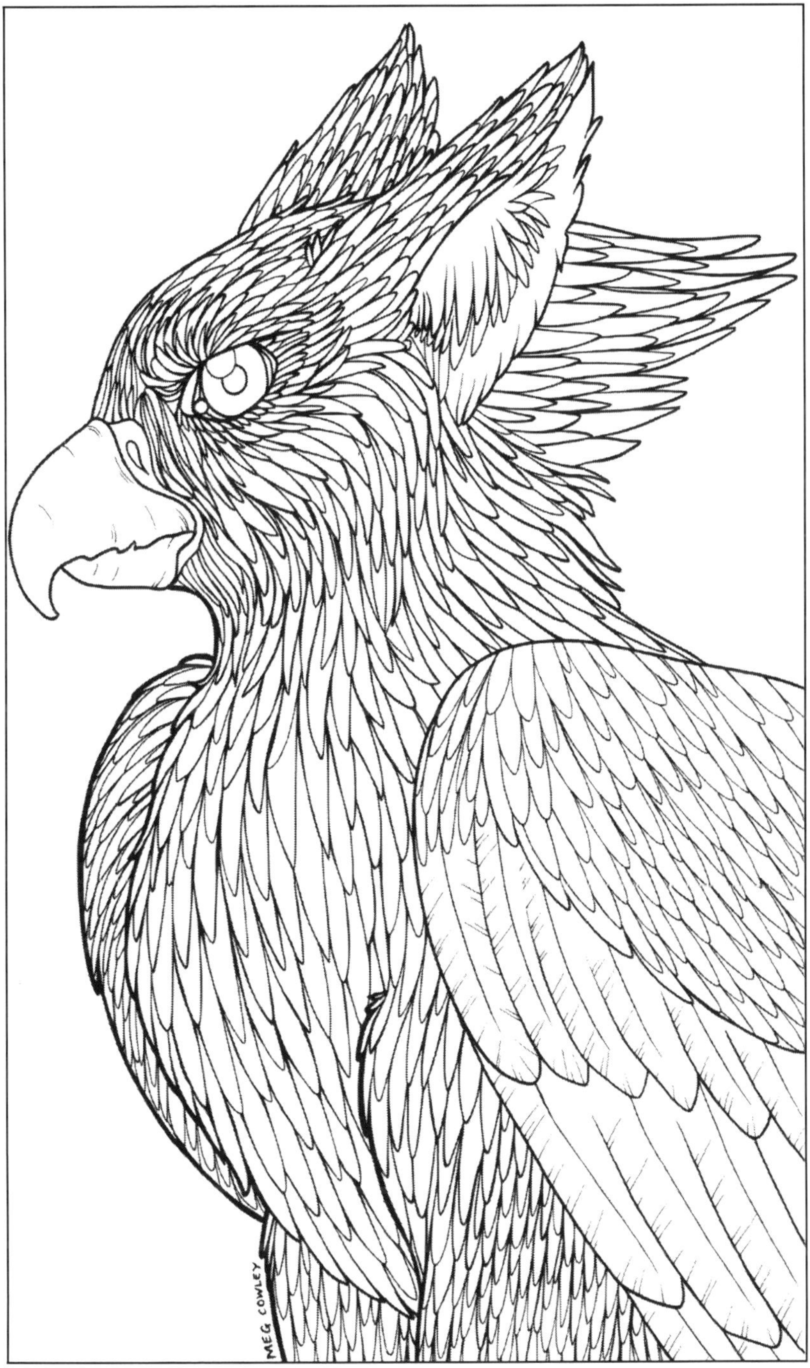
MEG COWLEY

Gryphon

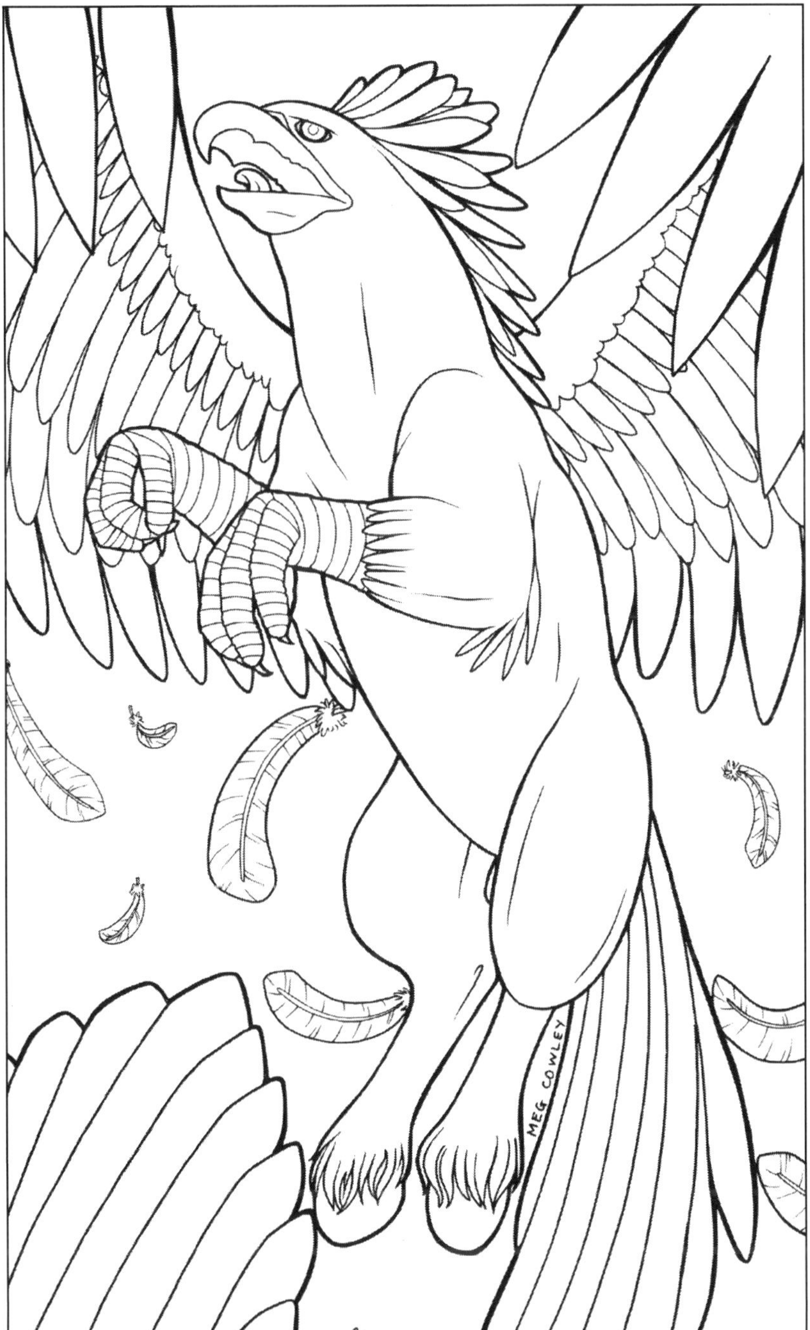
MEG COWLEY

Hippogriff

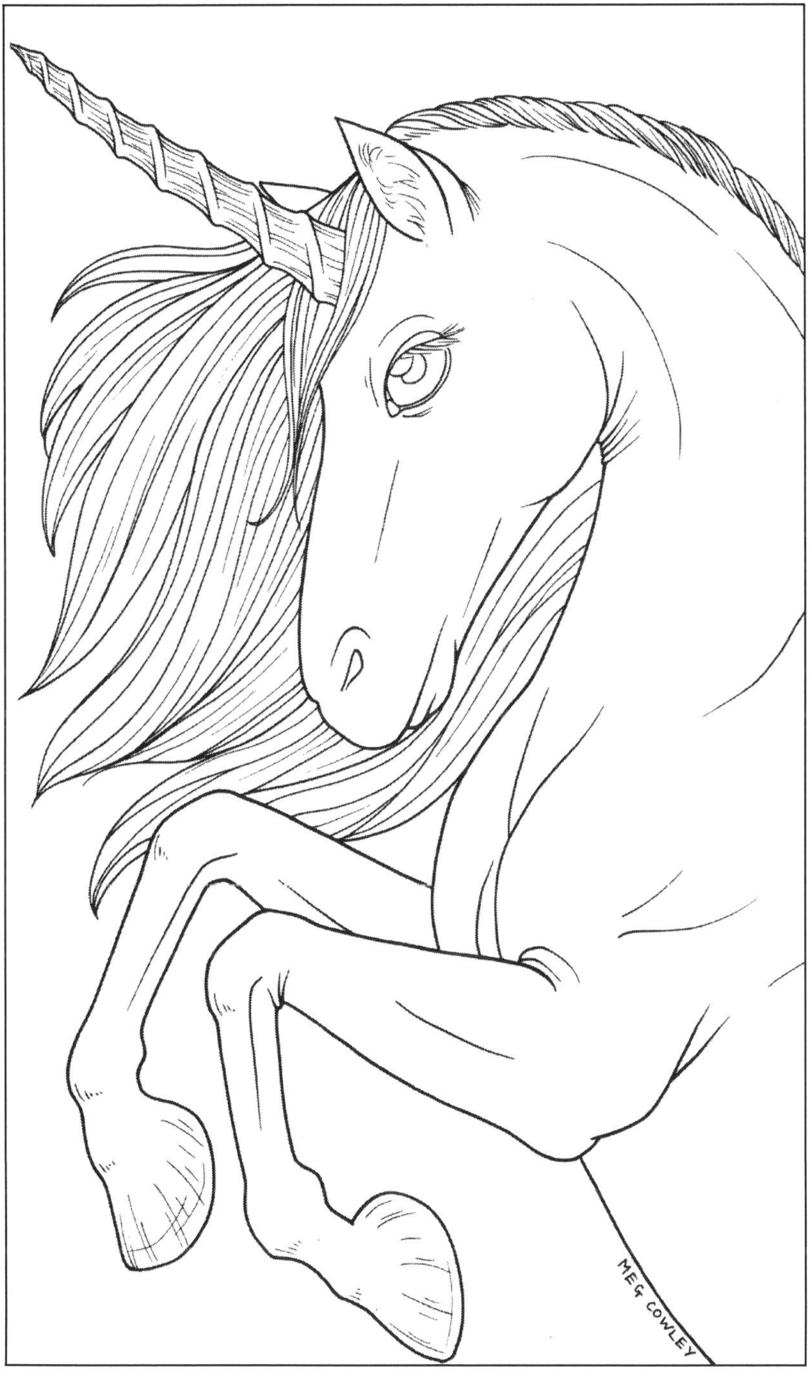
MEG COWLEY

Unicorn

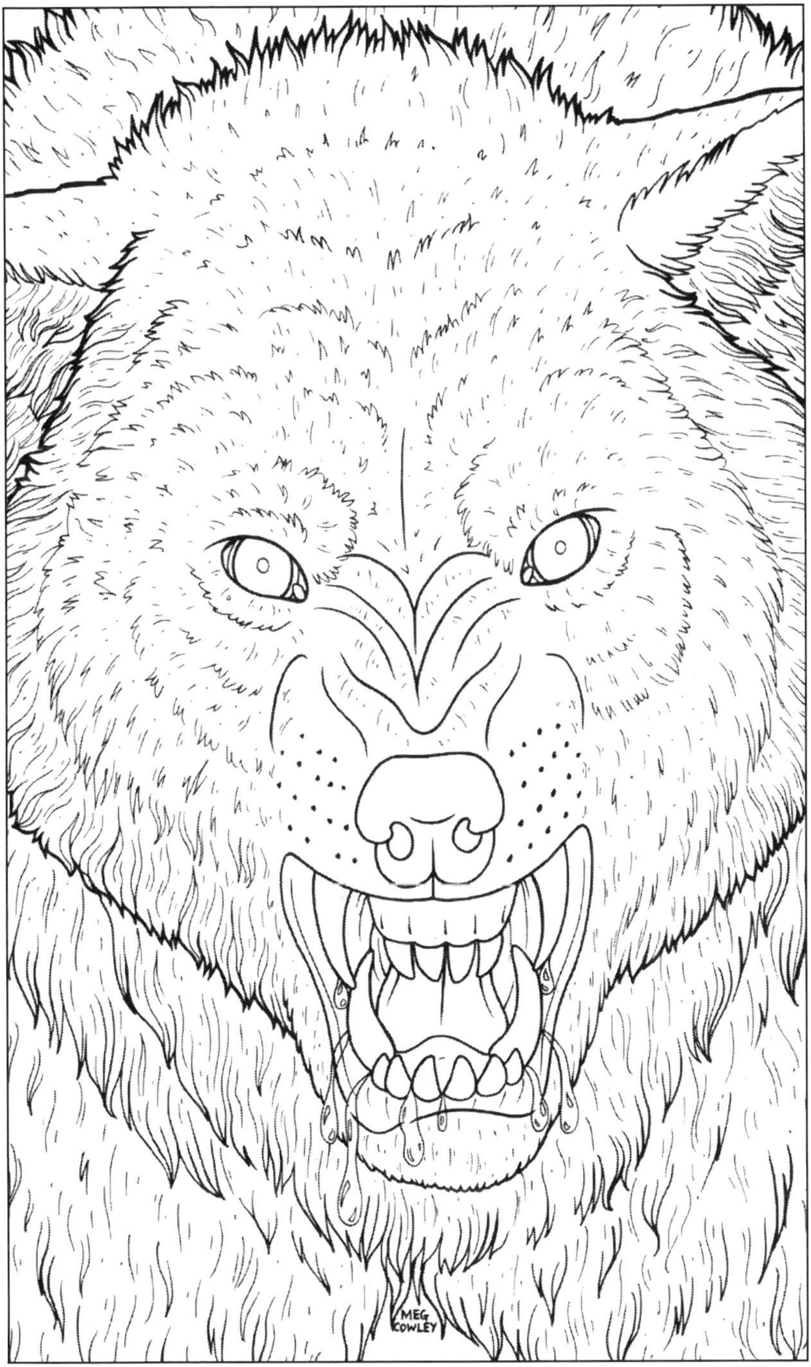
MEG
COWLEY

Grim

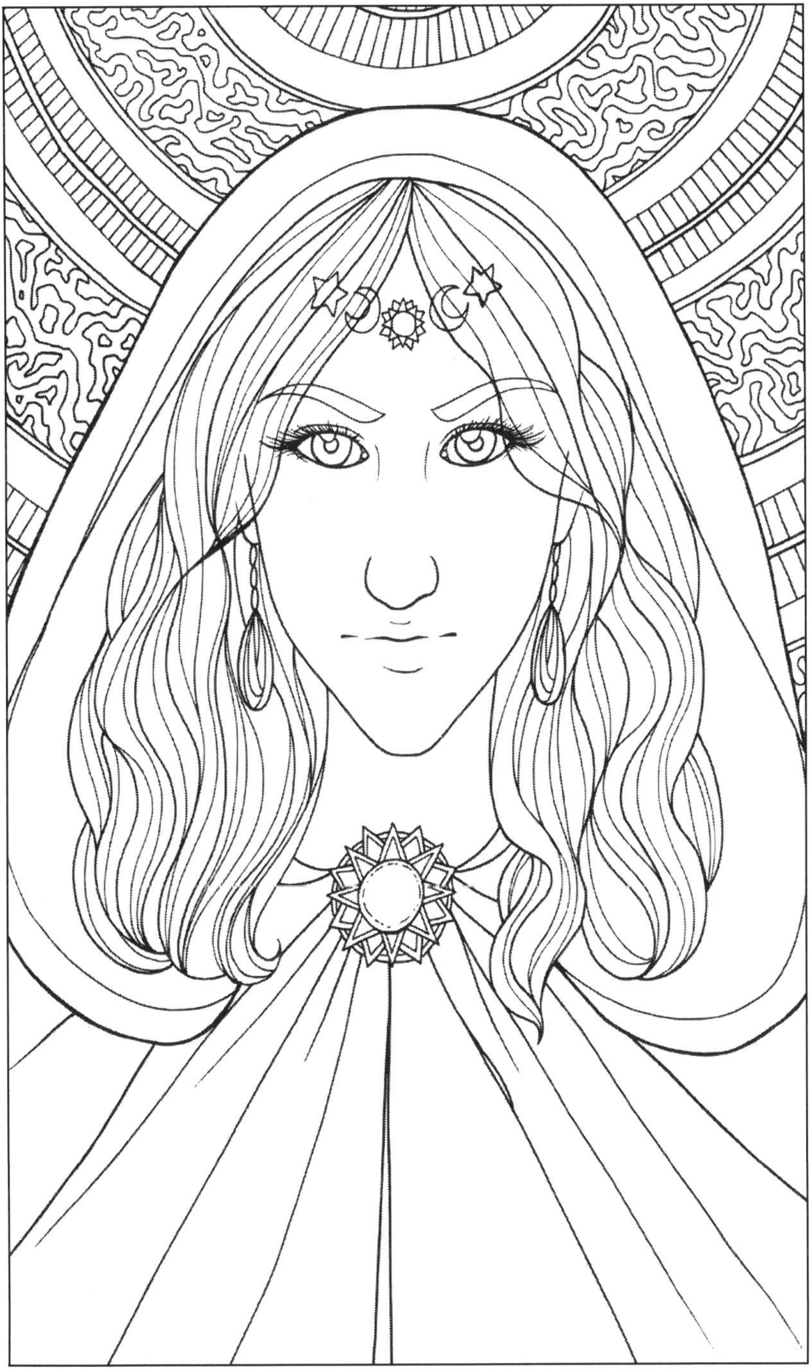

Witch

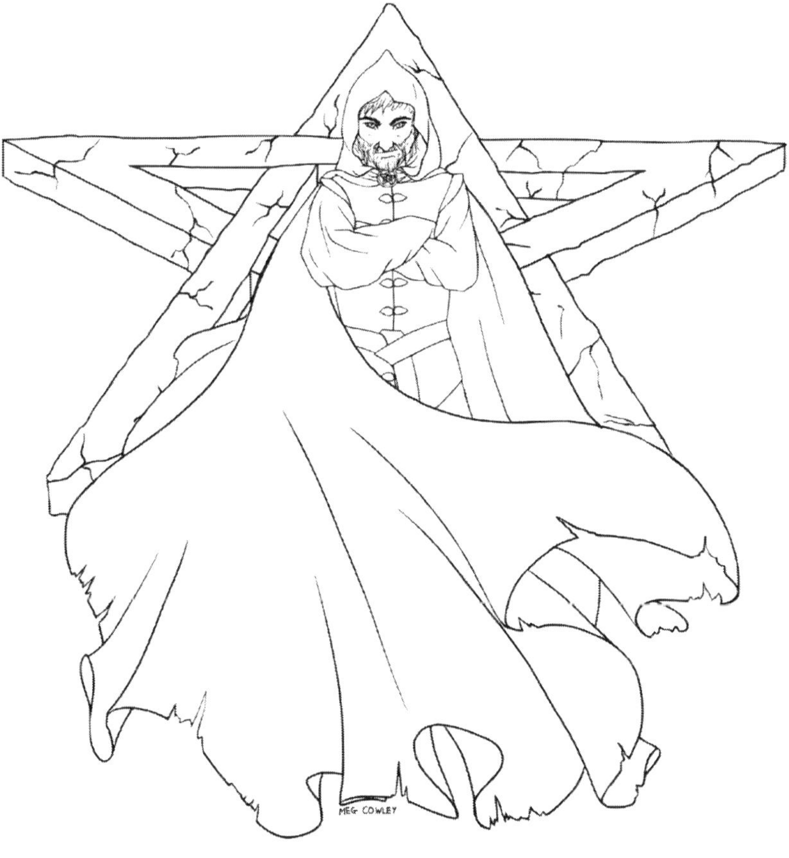
MEG COWLEY

Sorcerer

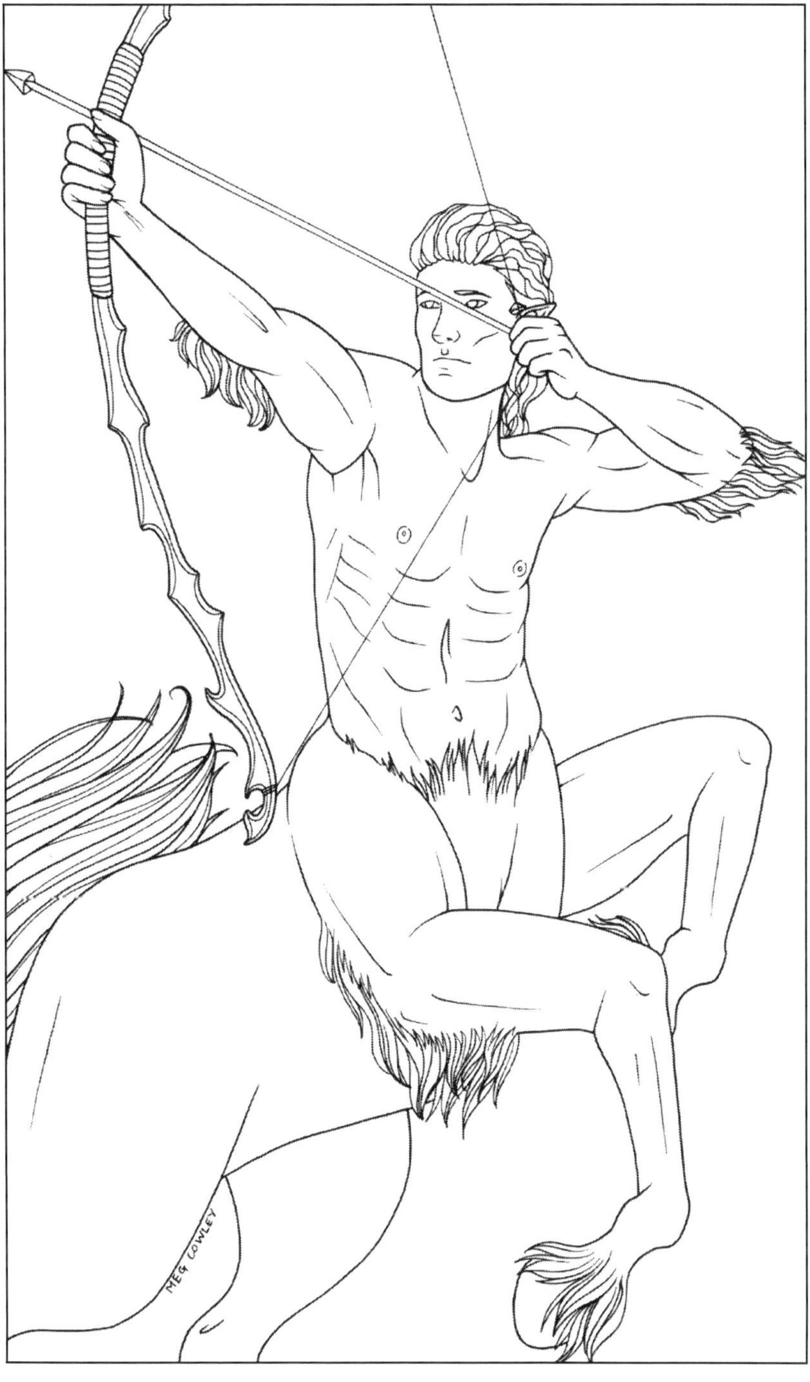
MEG COWLEY

Centaur

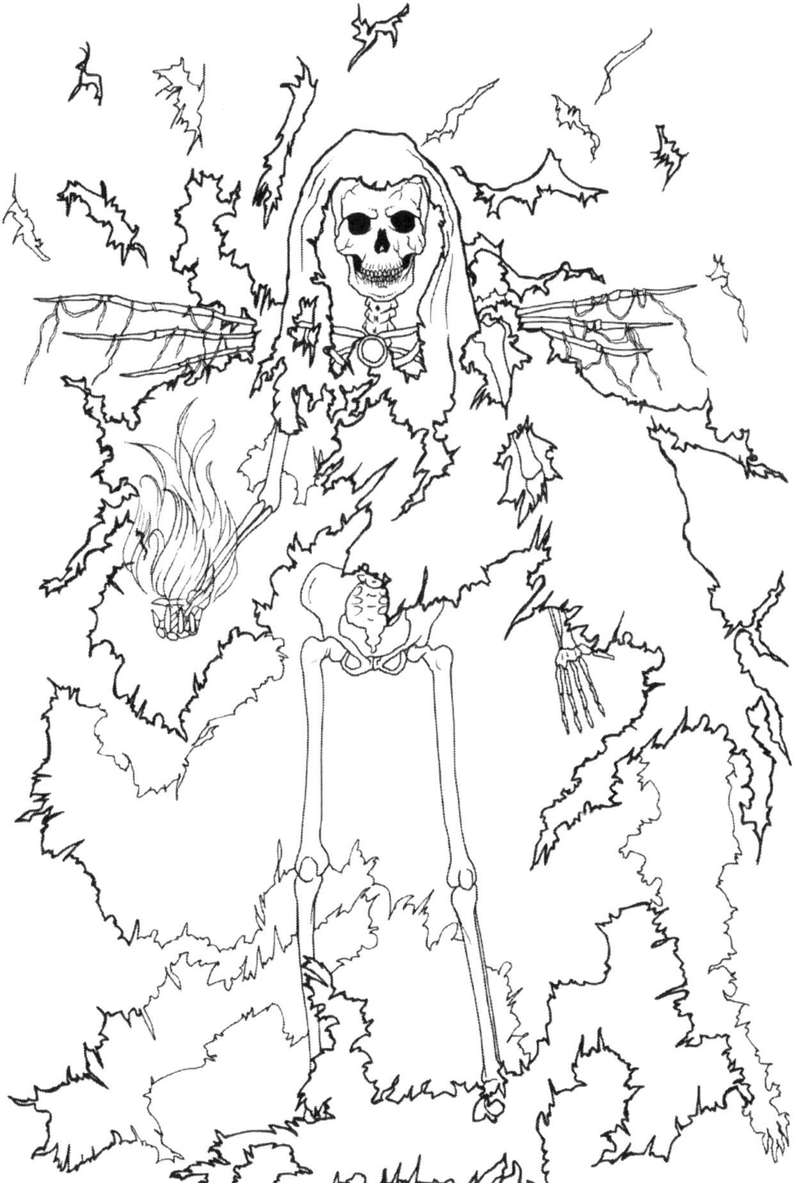
MEG COWLEY

Revenant

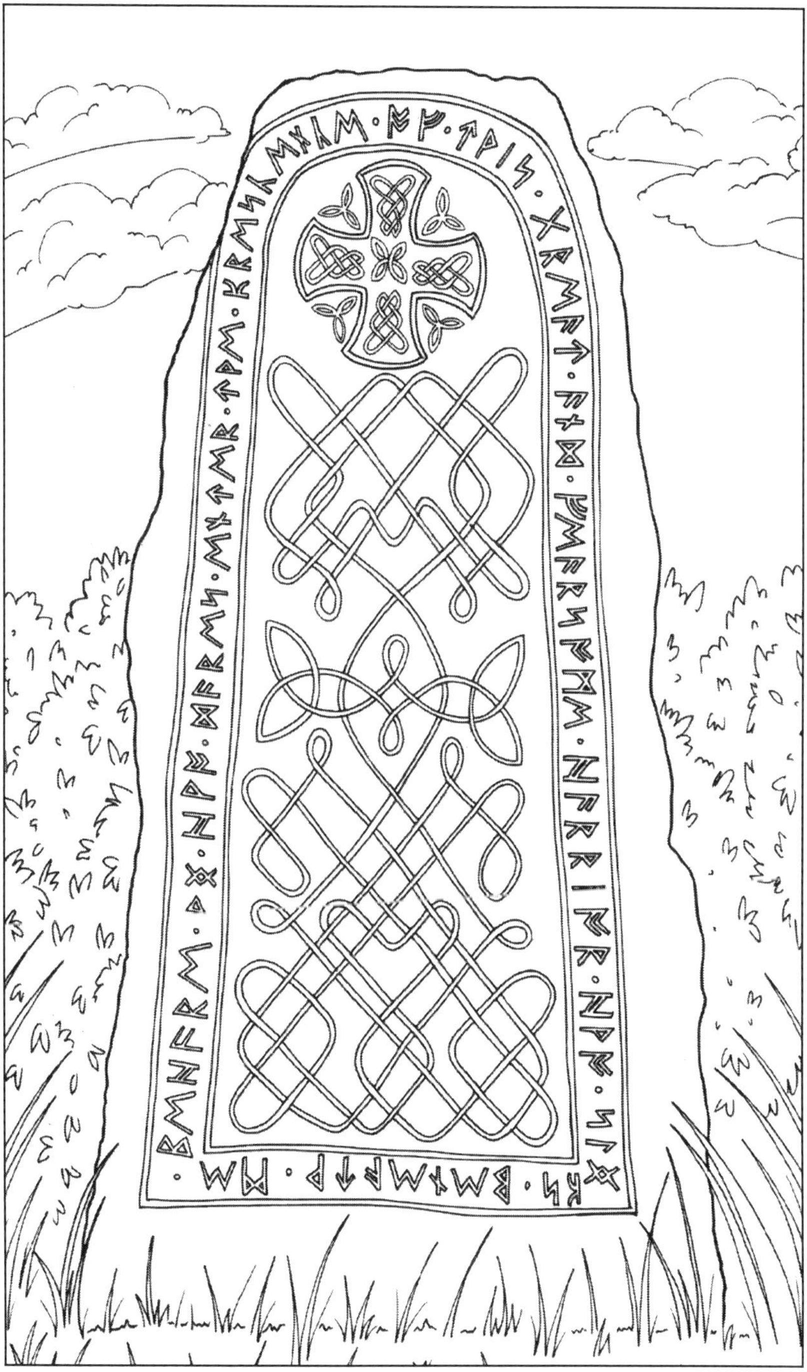

Rune Stone

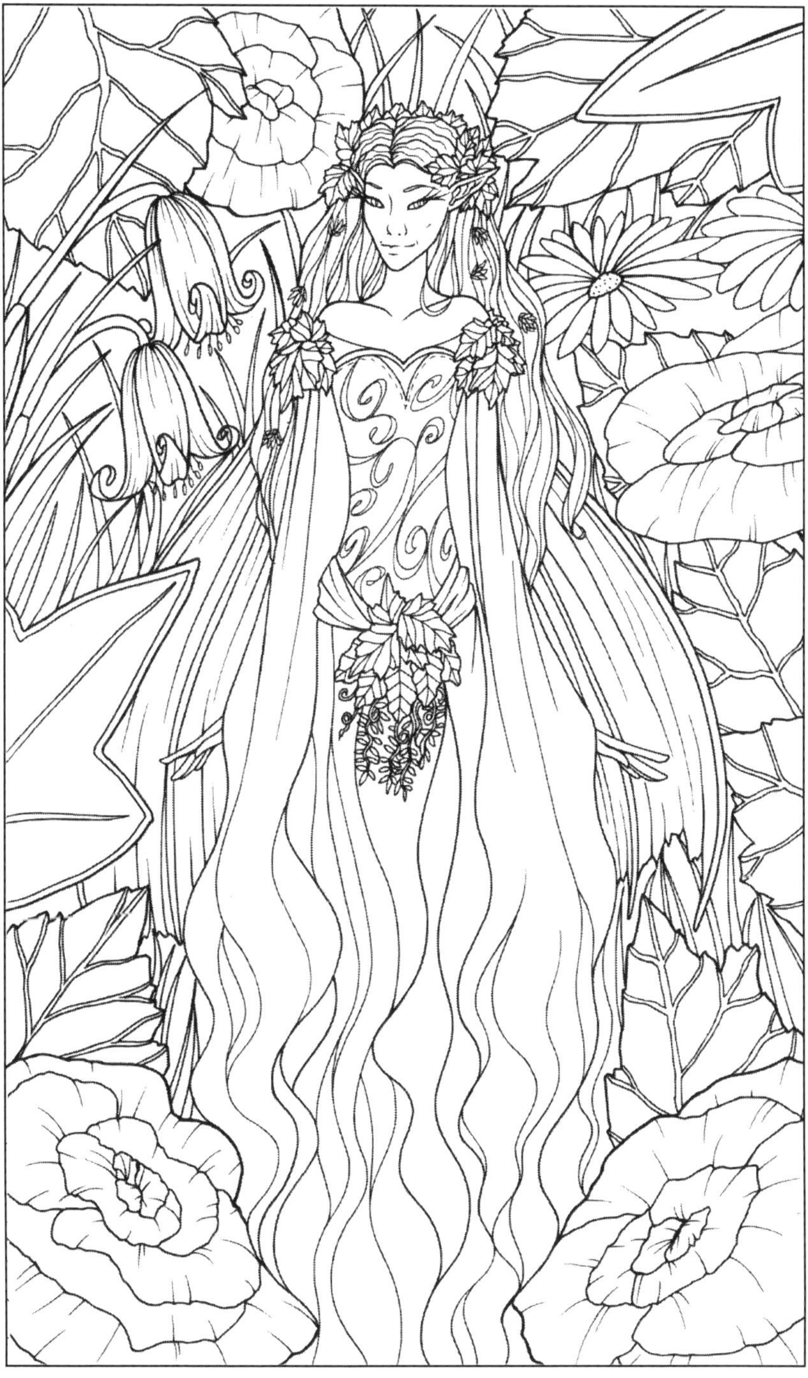

Faerie Queen

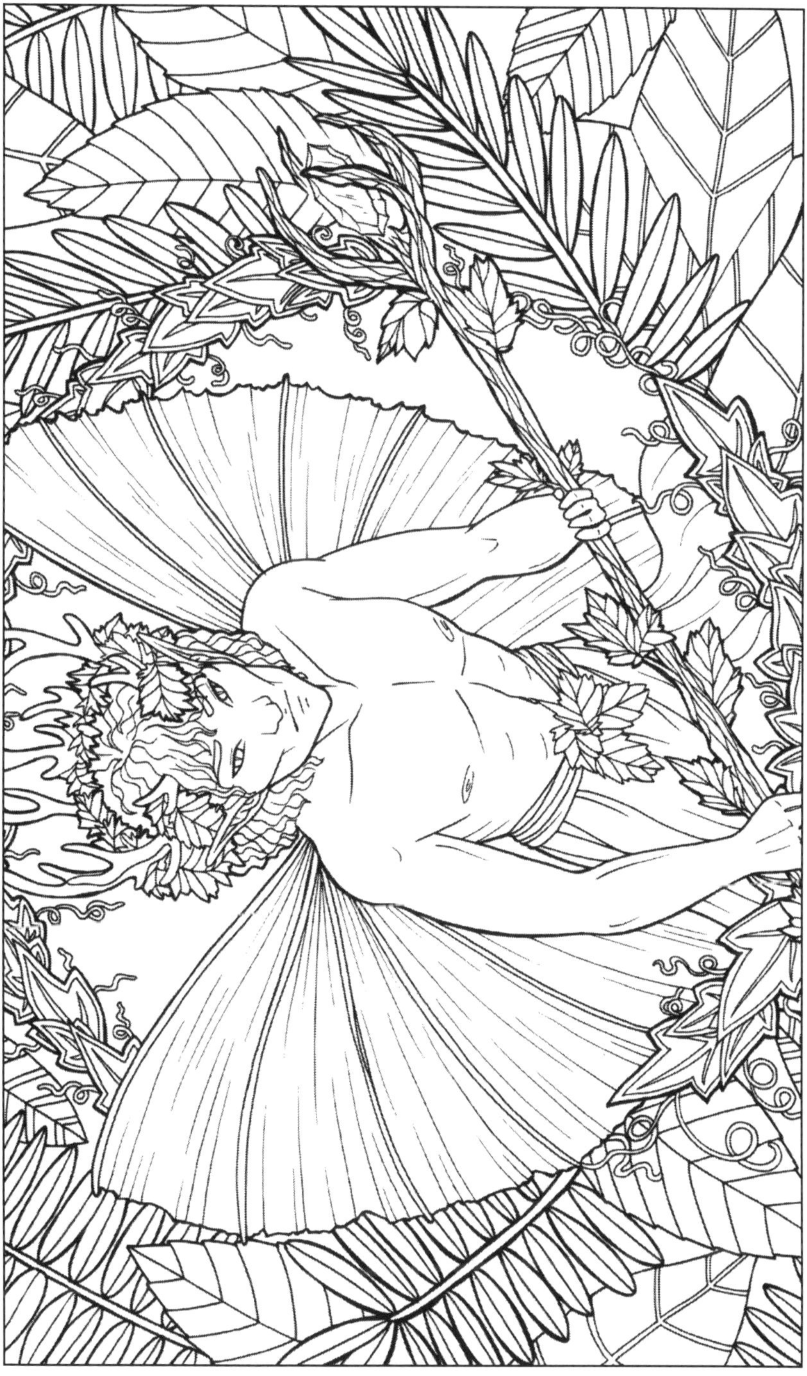

Faerie King

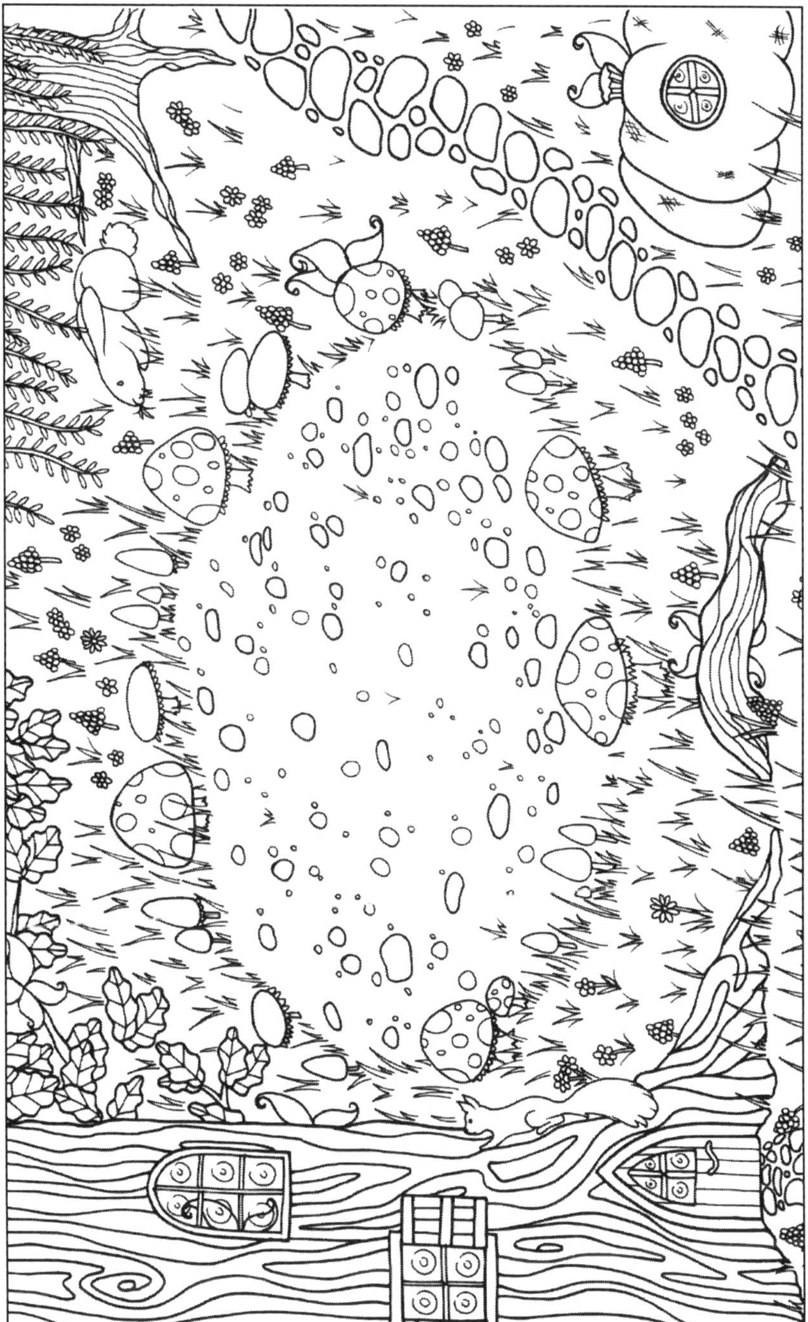

Faerie Circle

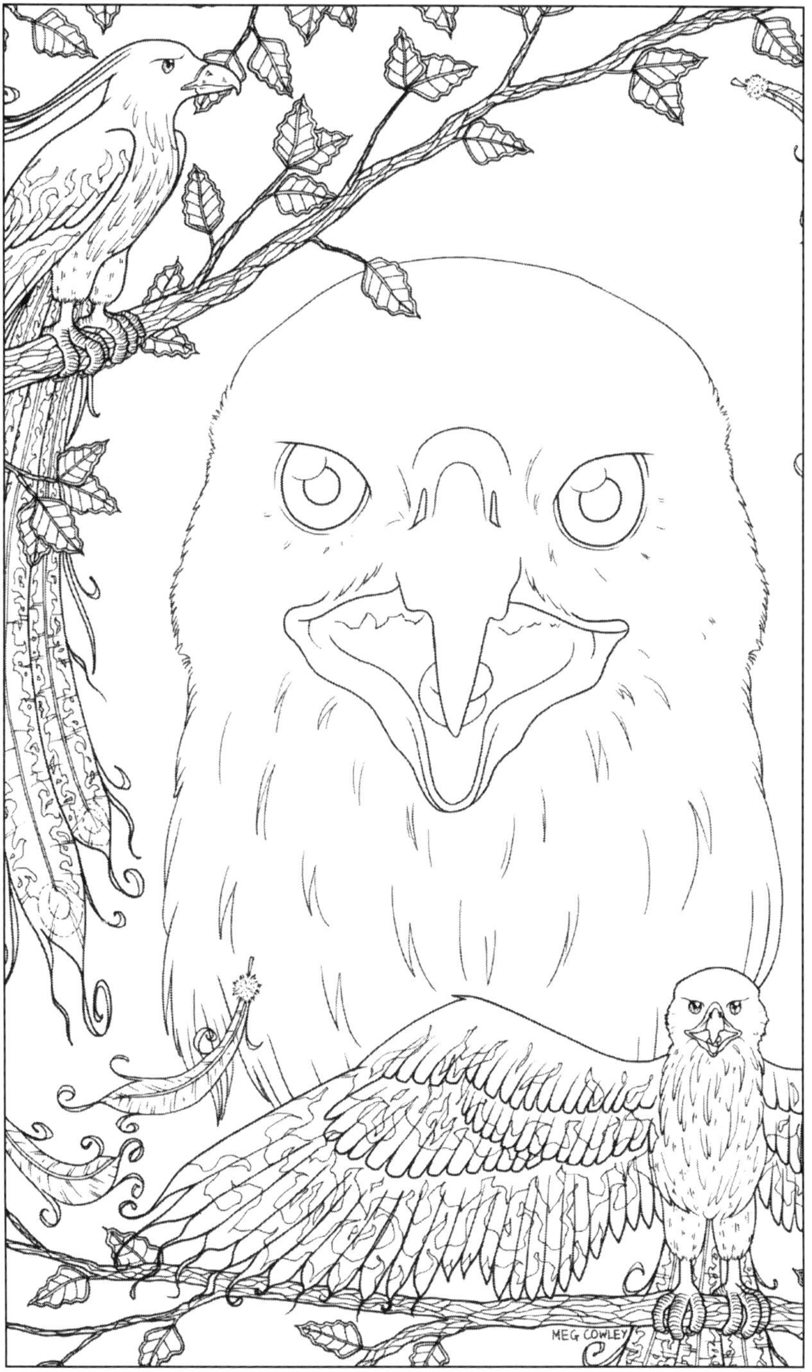
MEG COWLEY

Phoenix

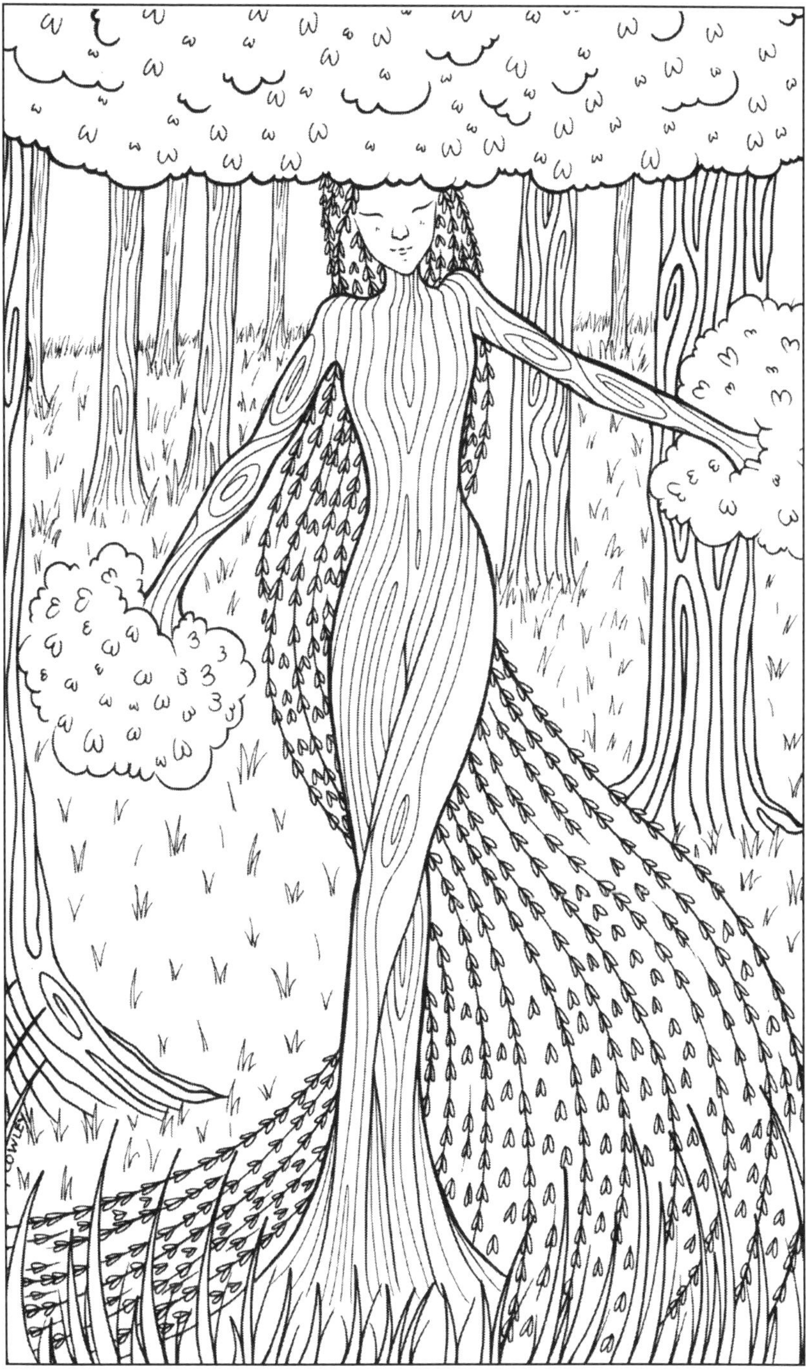

Dryad

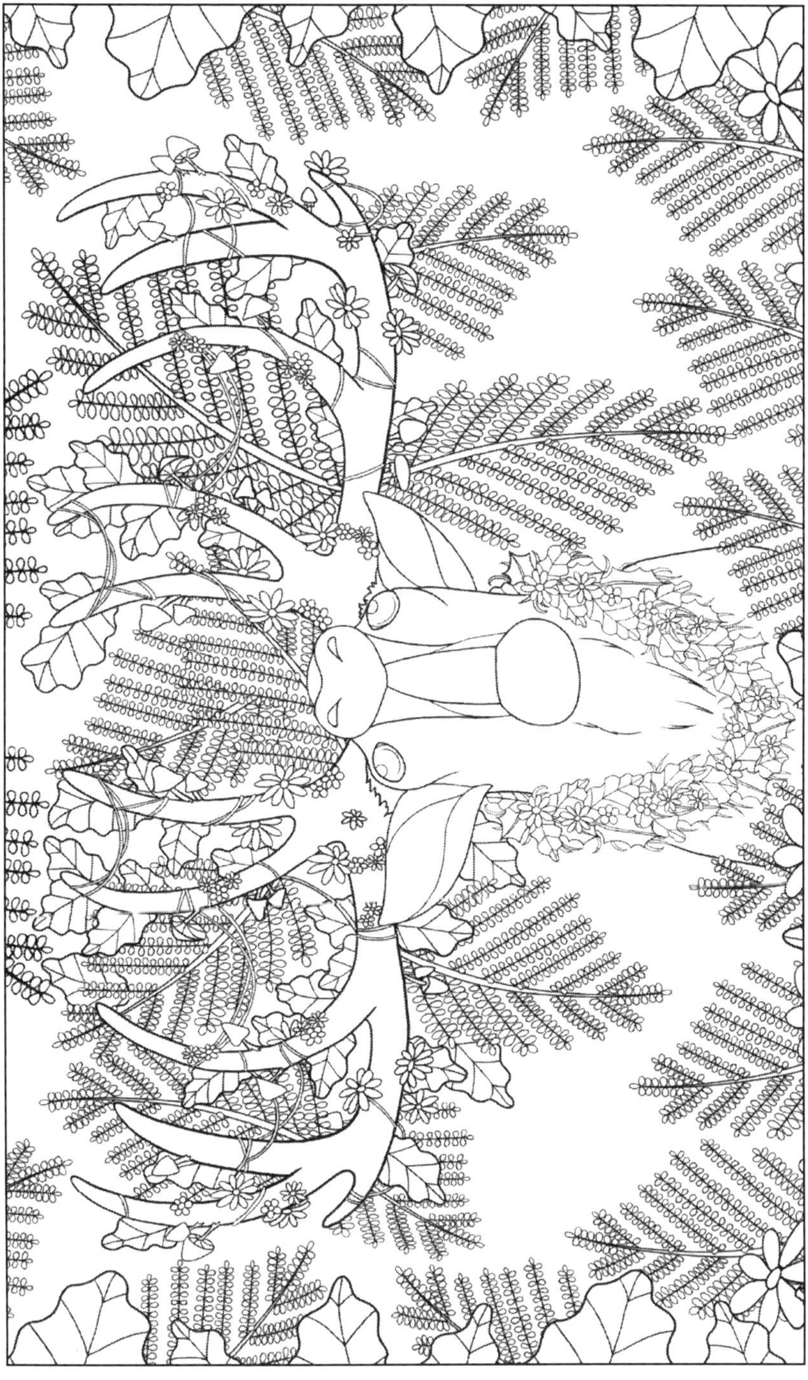

King of the Forest

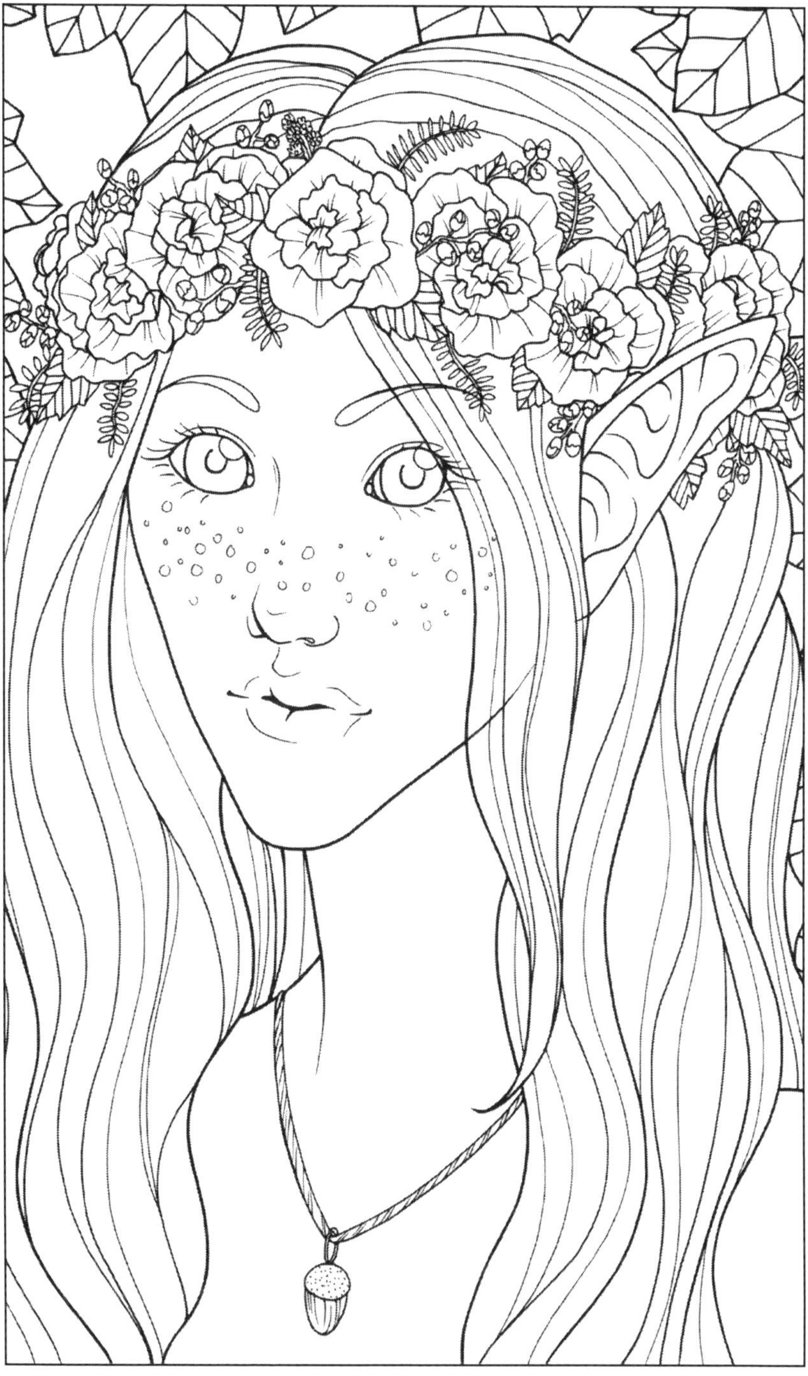

Elf

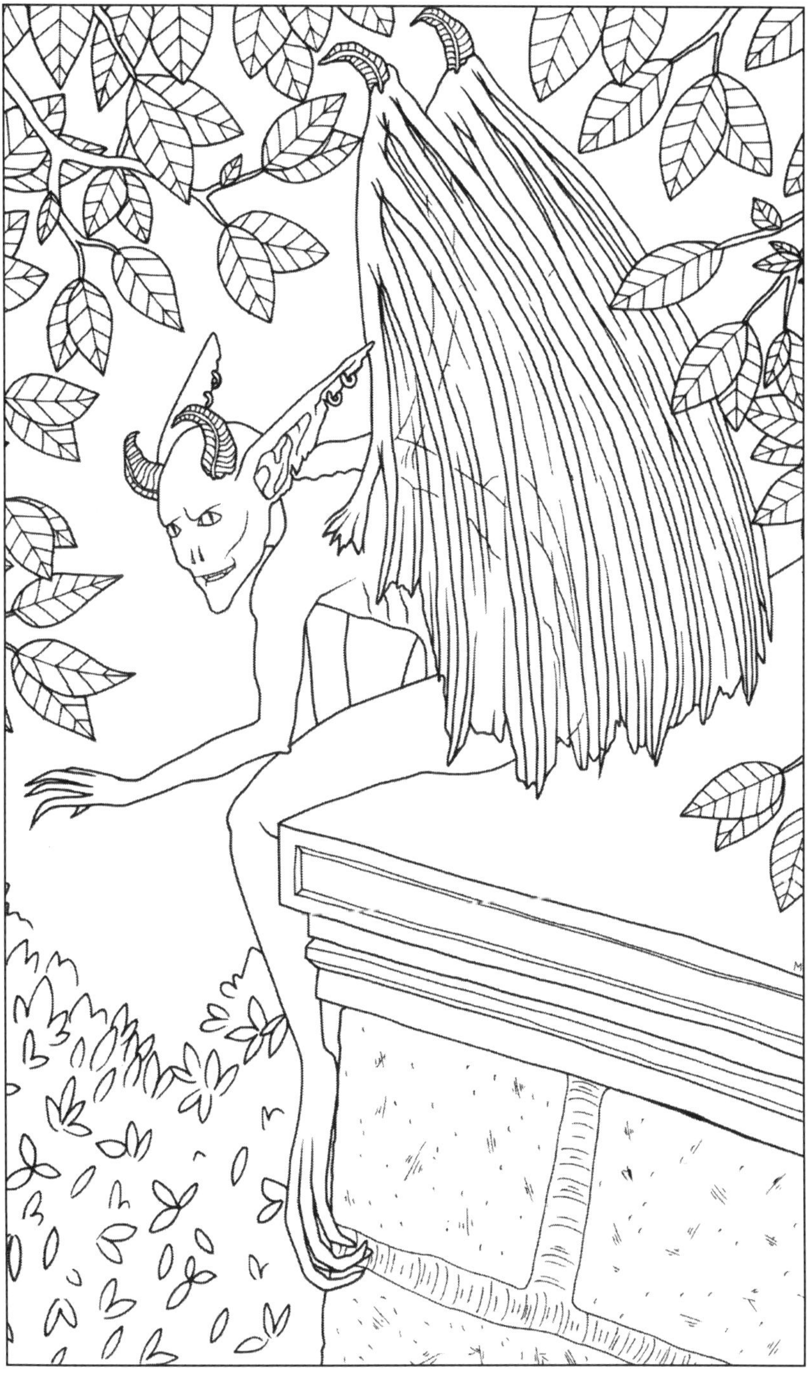

Imp

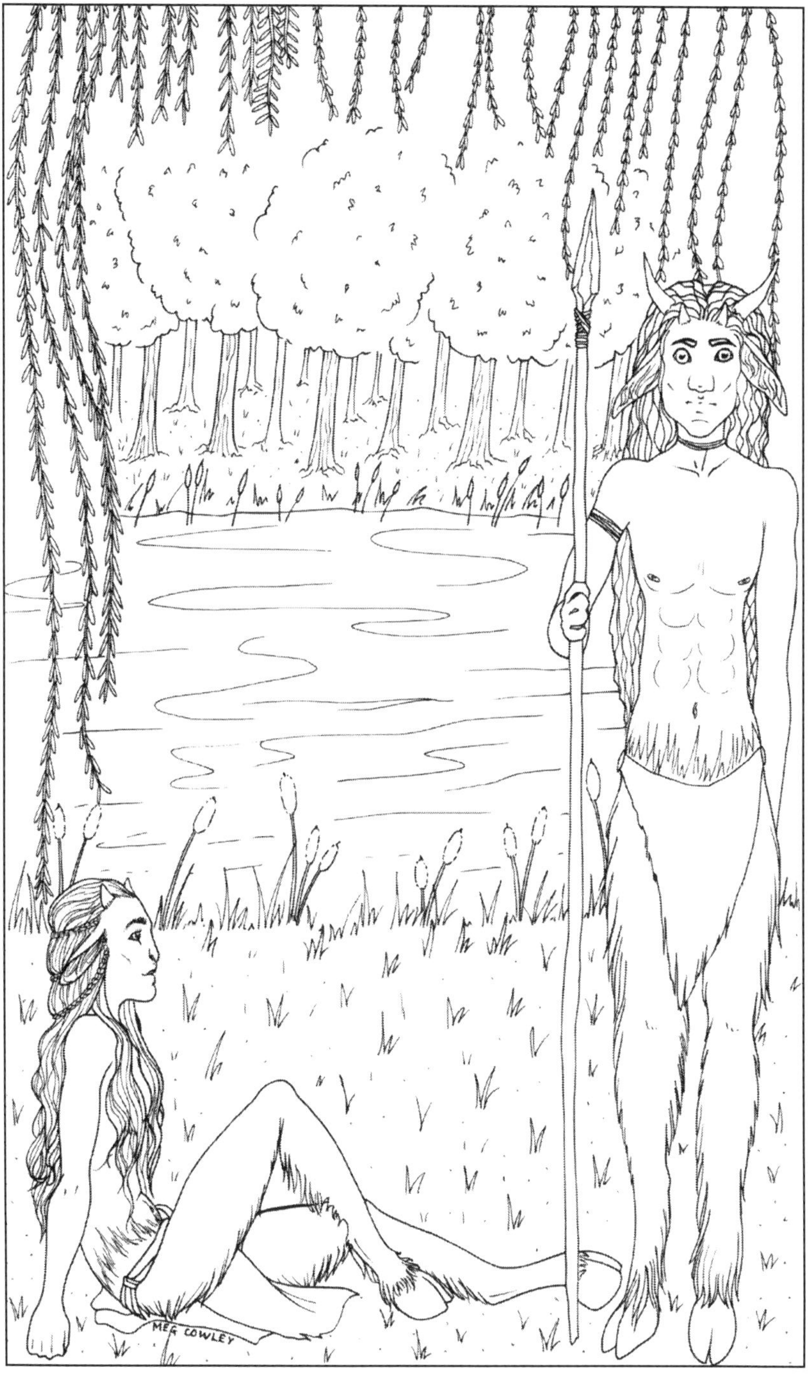
MEG COWLEY

Faun

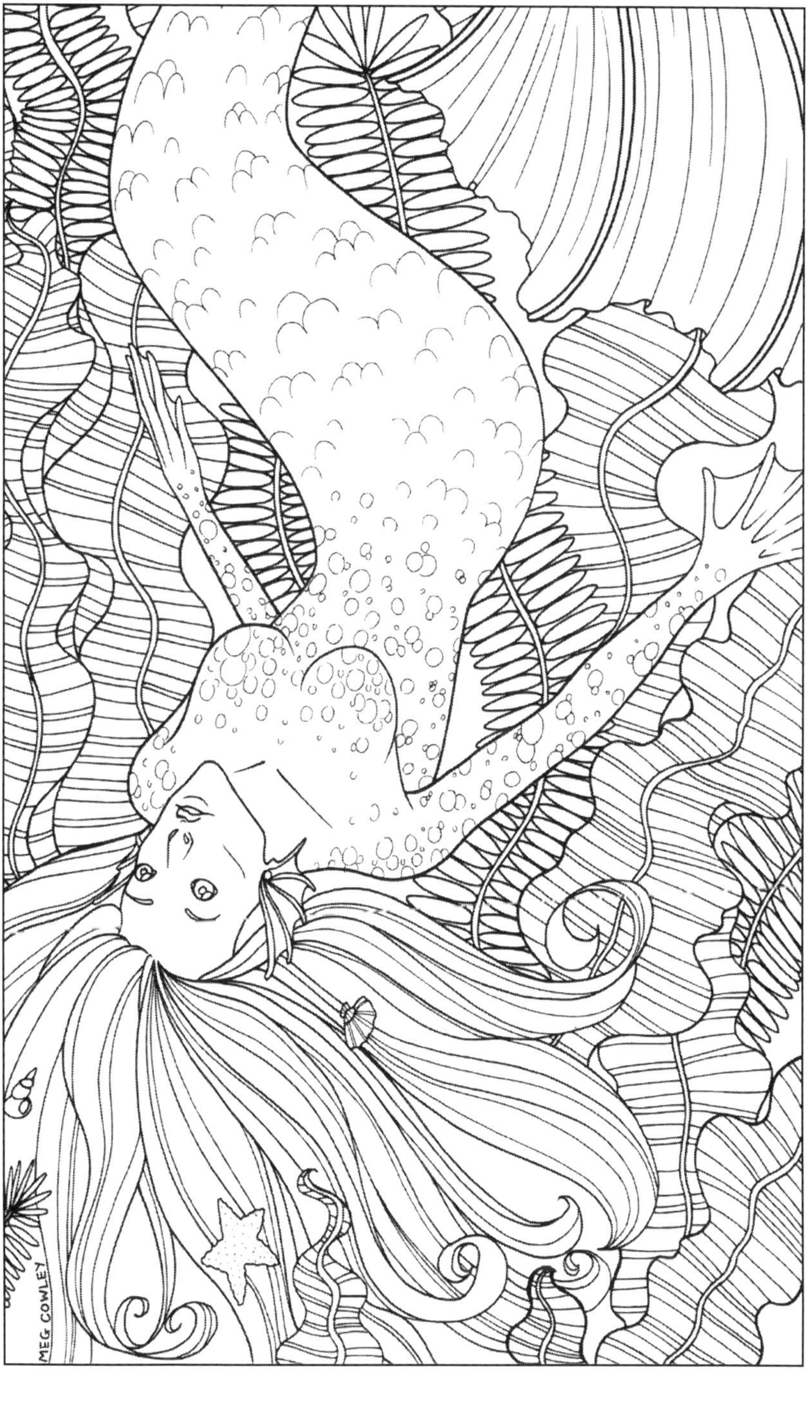
MEG COWLEY

Mermaid

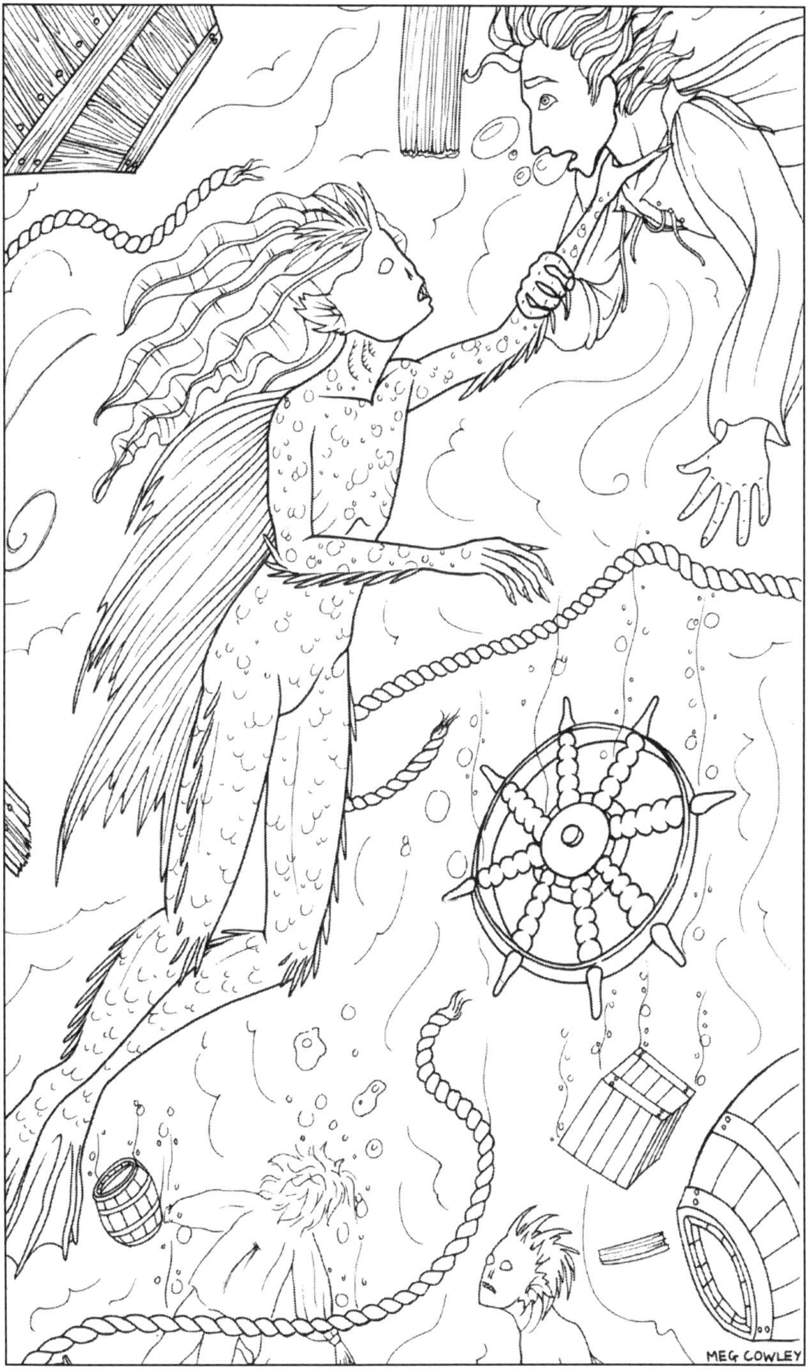
MEG COWLEY

Siren

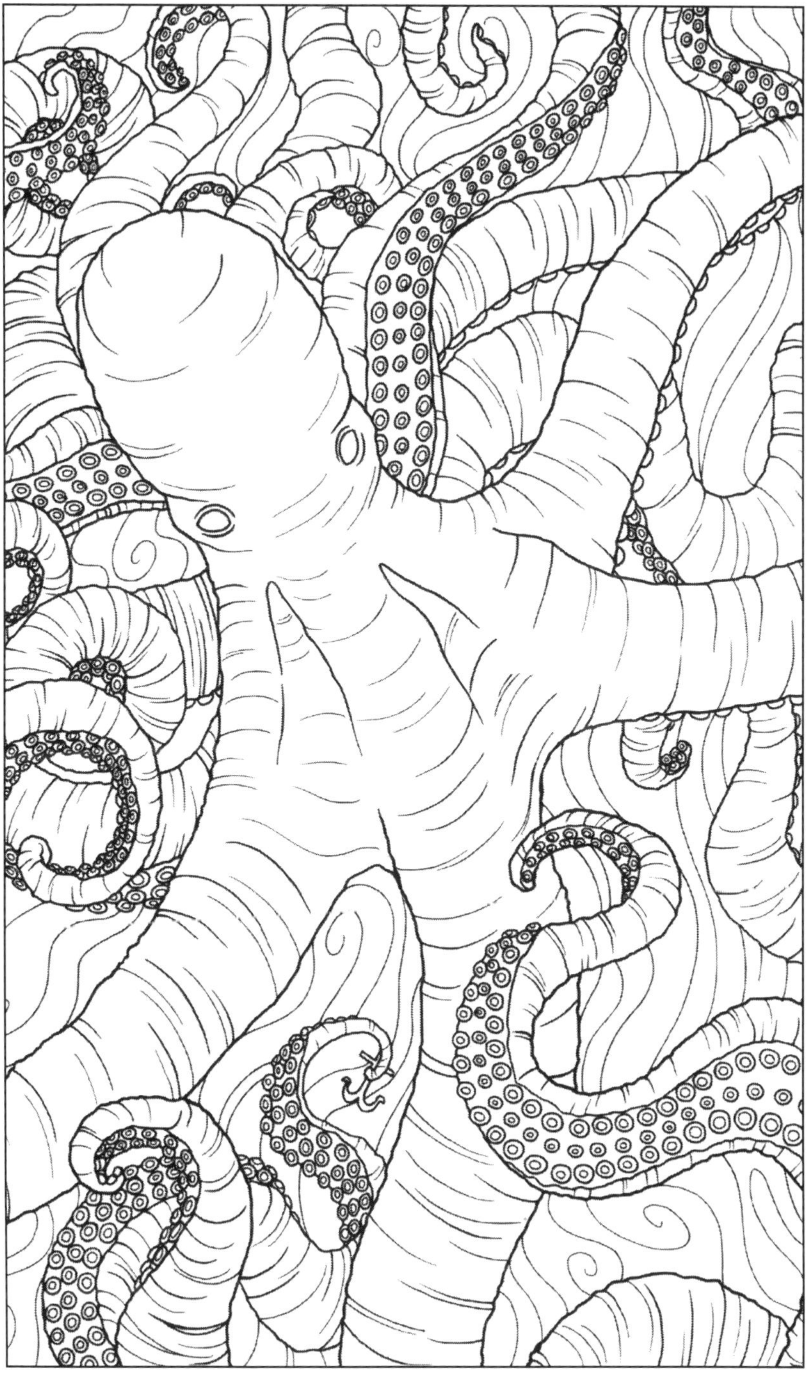

Kraken

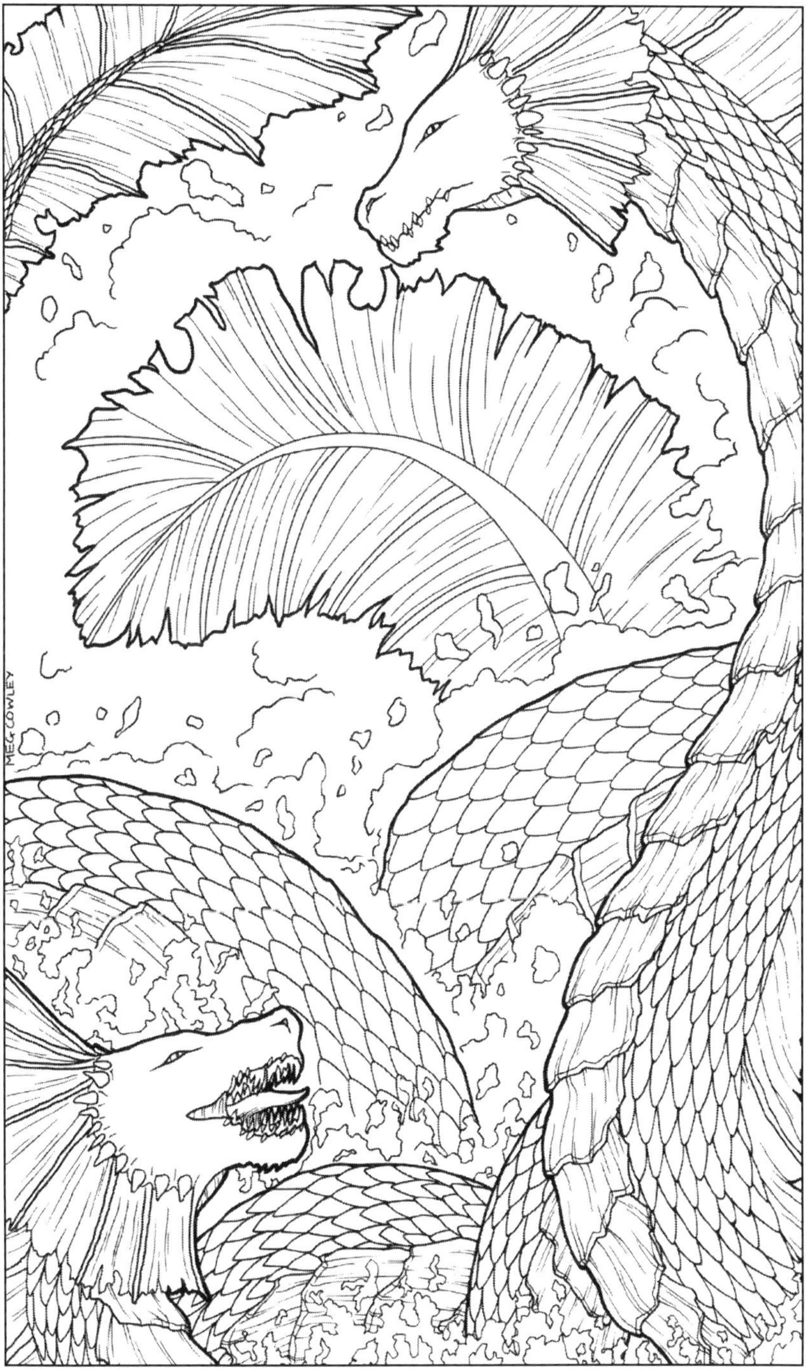
MEG COWLEY

Knucker

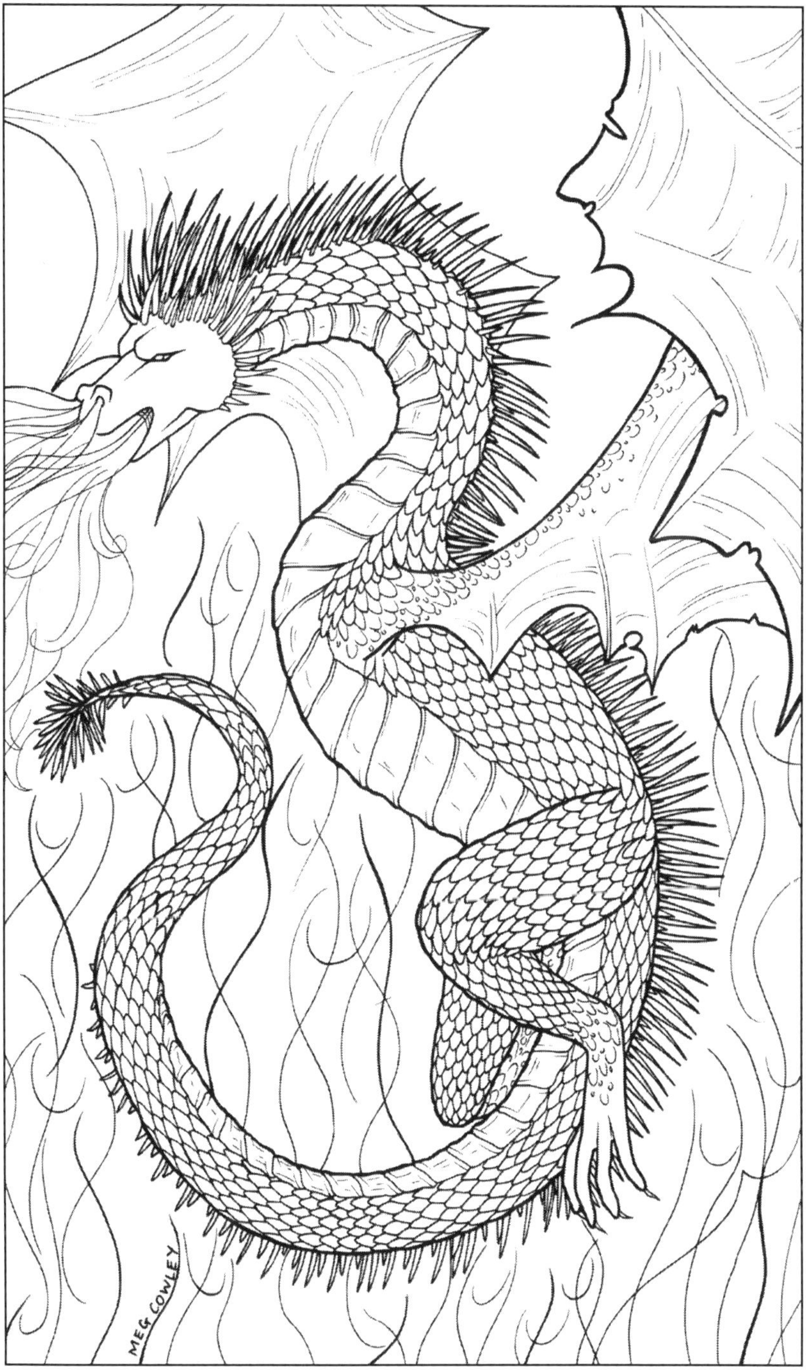
MEG COWLEY

Wyvern

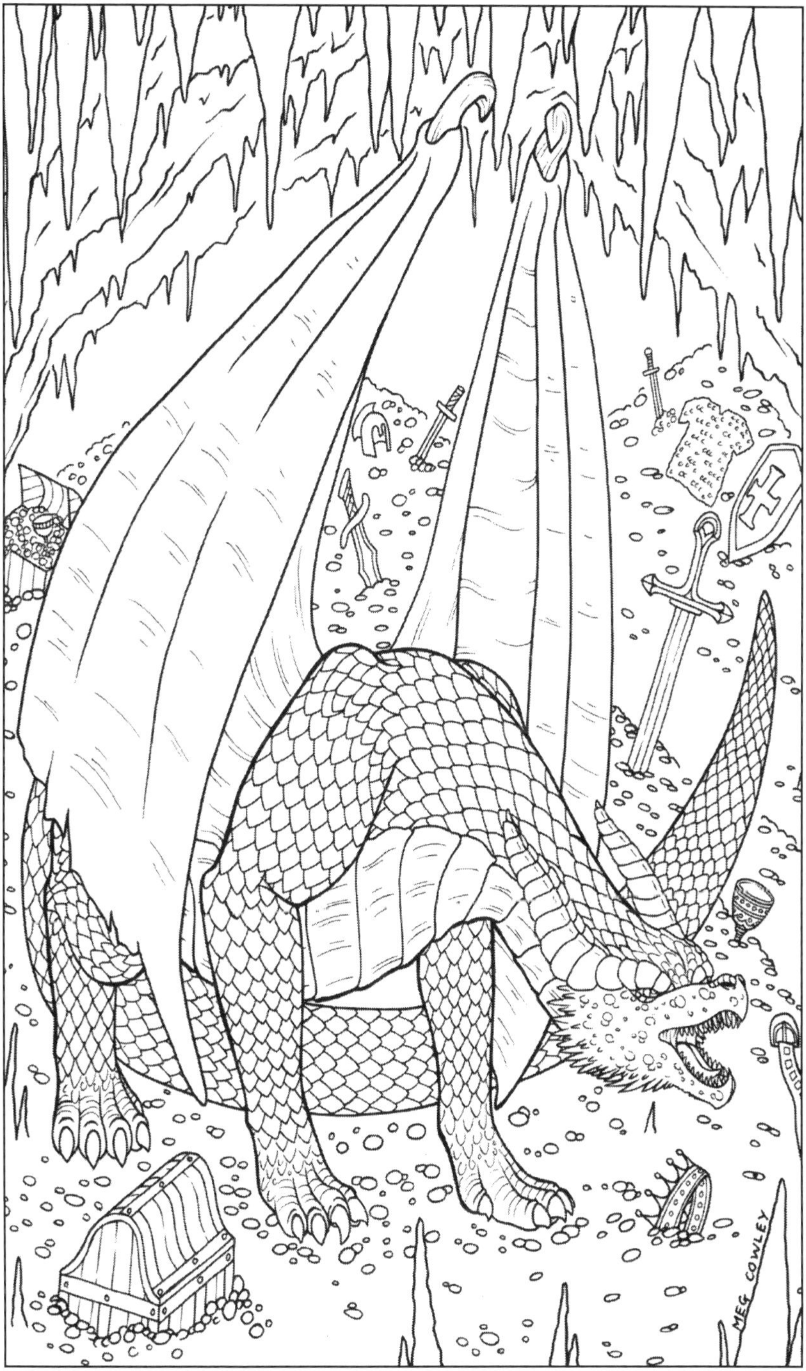
MEG COWLEY

Dragon

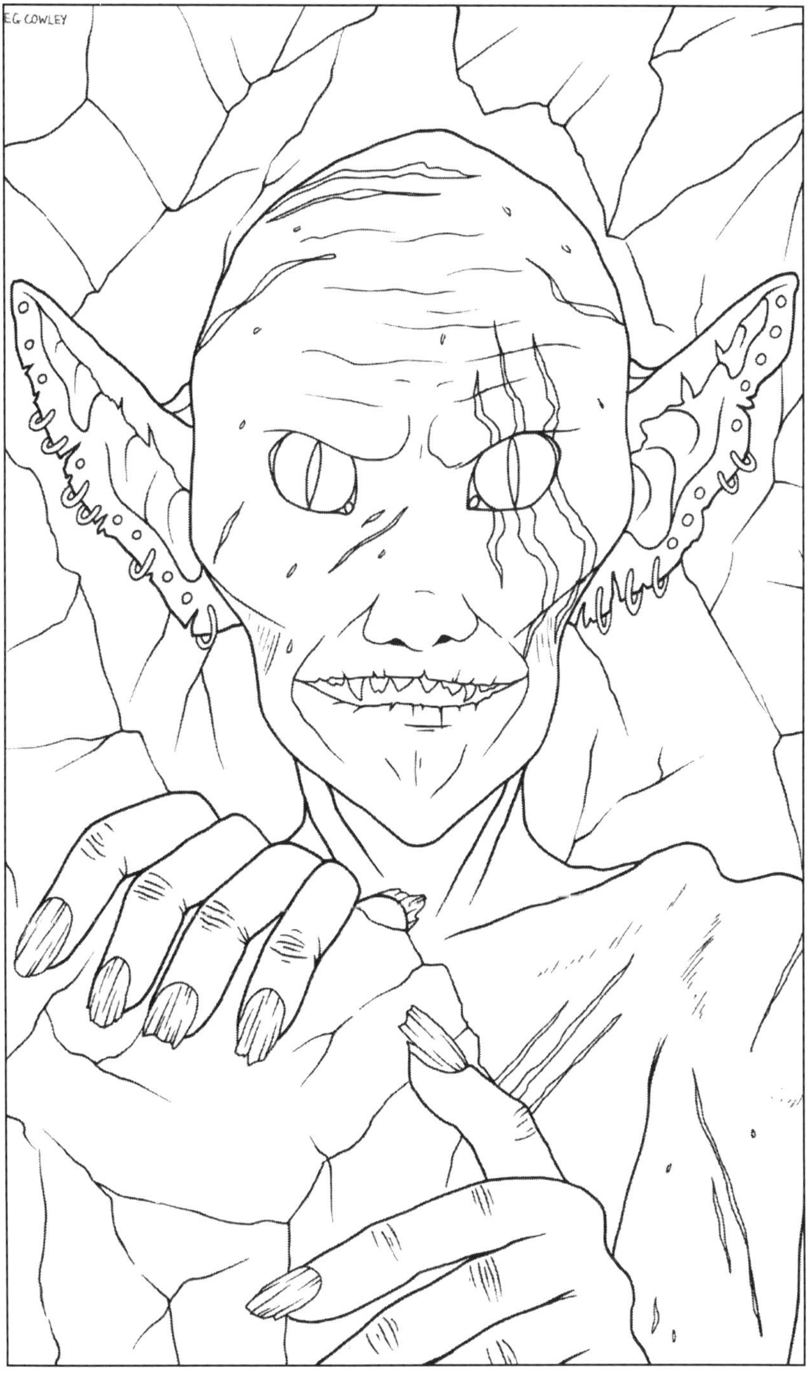
E.G. COWLEY

Goblin

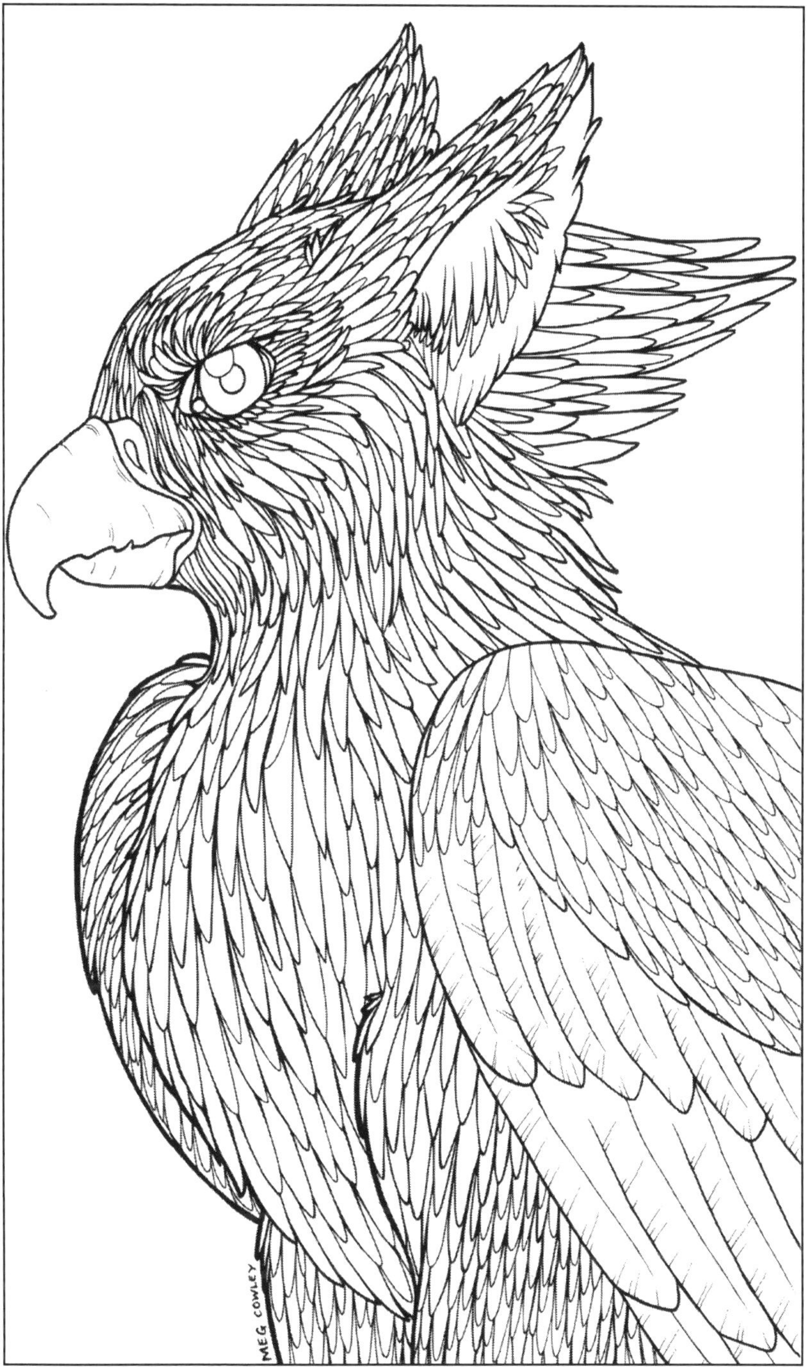
MEG COWLEY

Gryphon

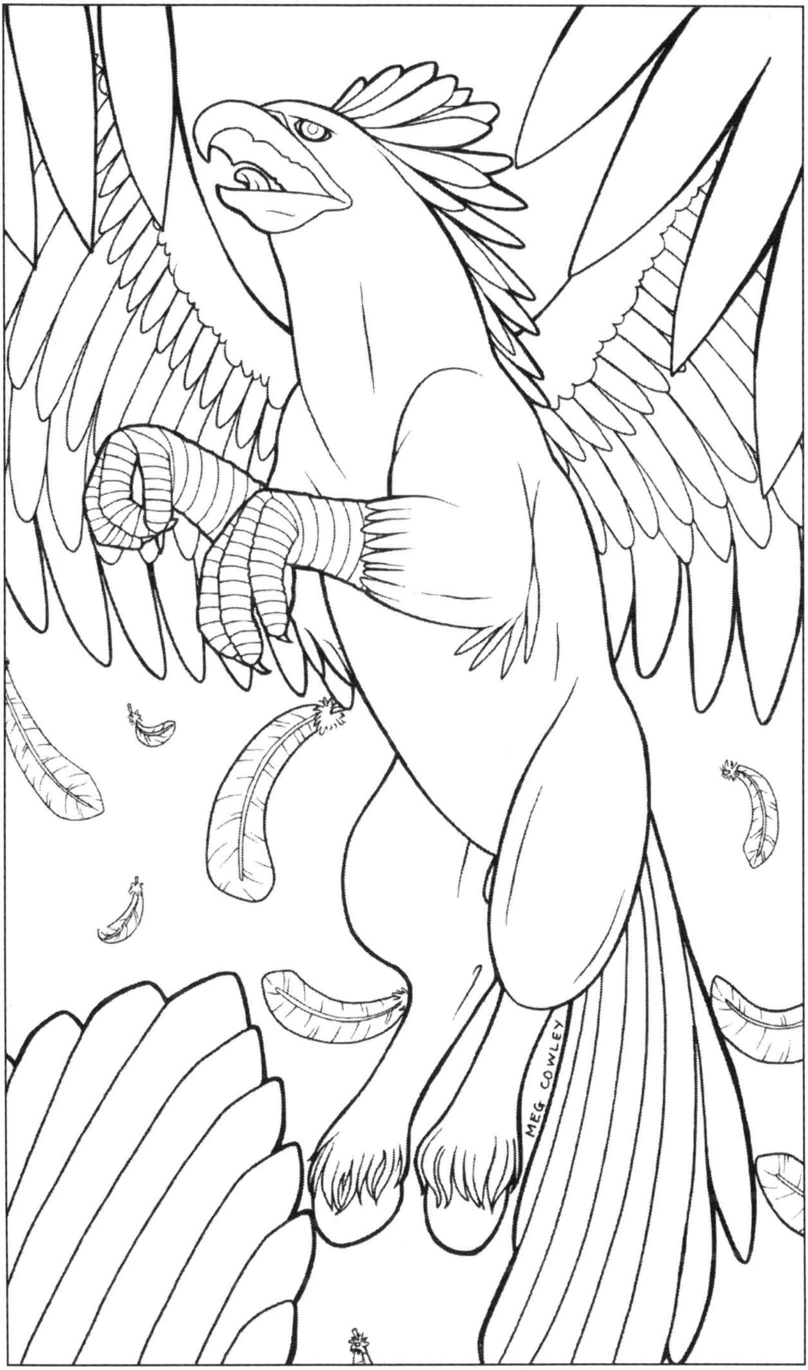
MEG COWLEY

Hippogriff

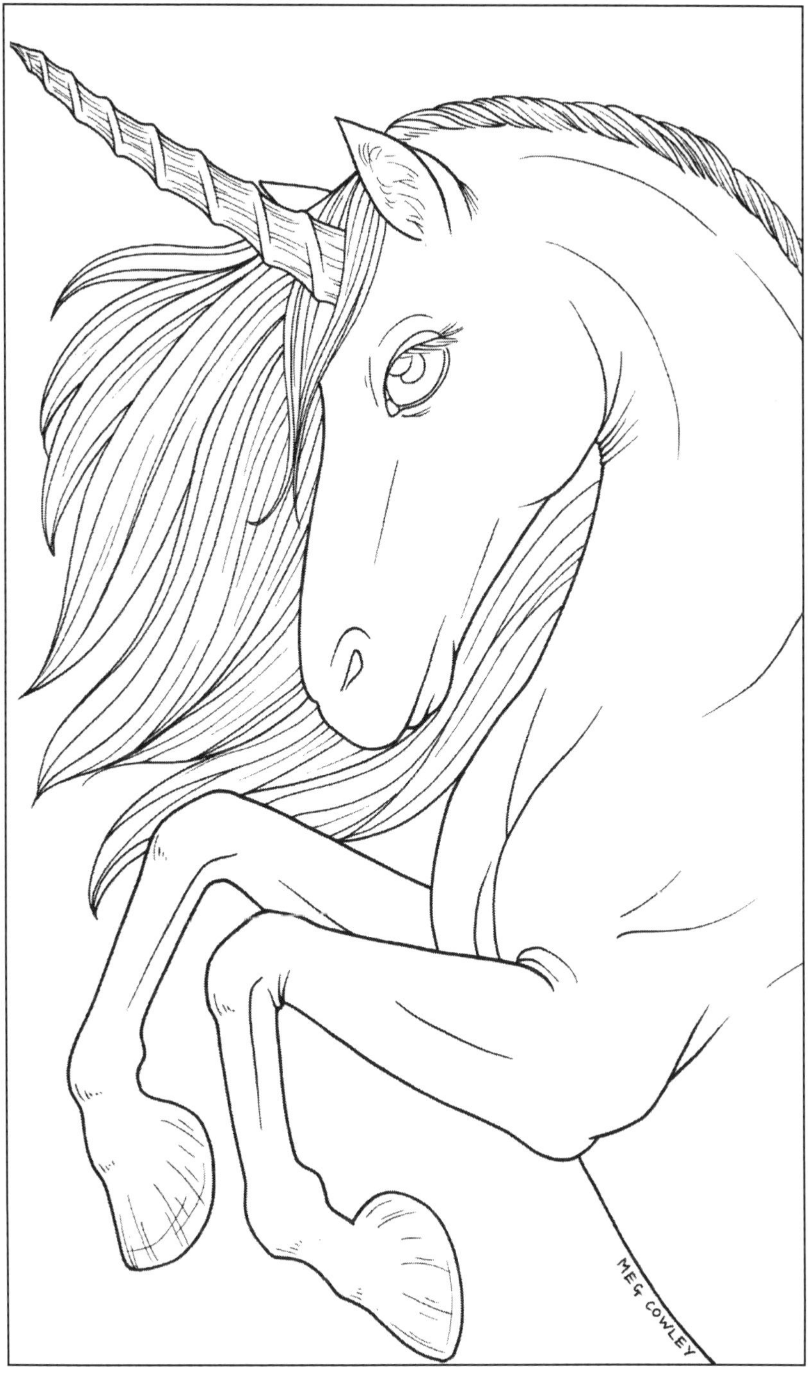
MEG COWLEY

Unicorn

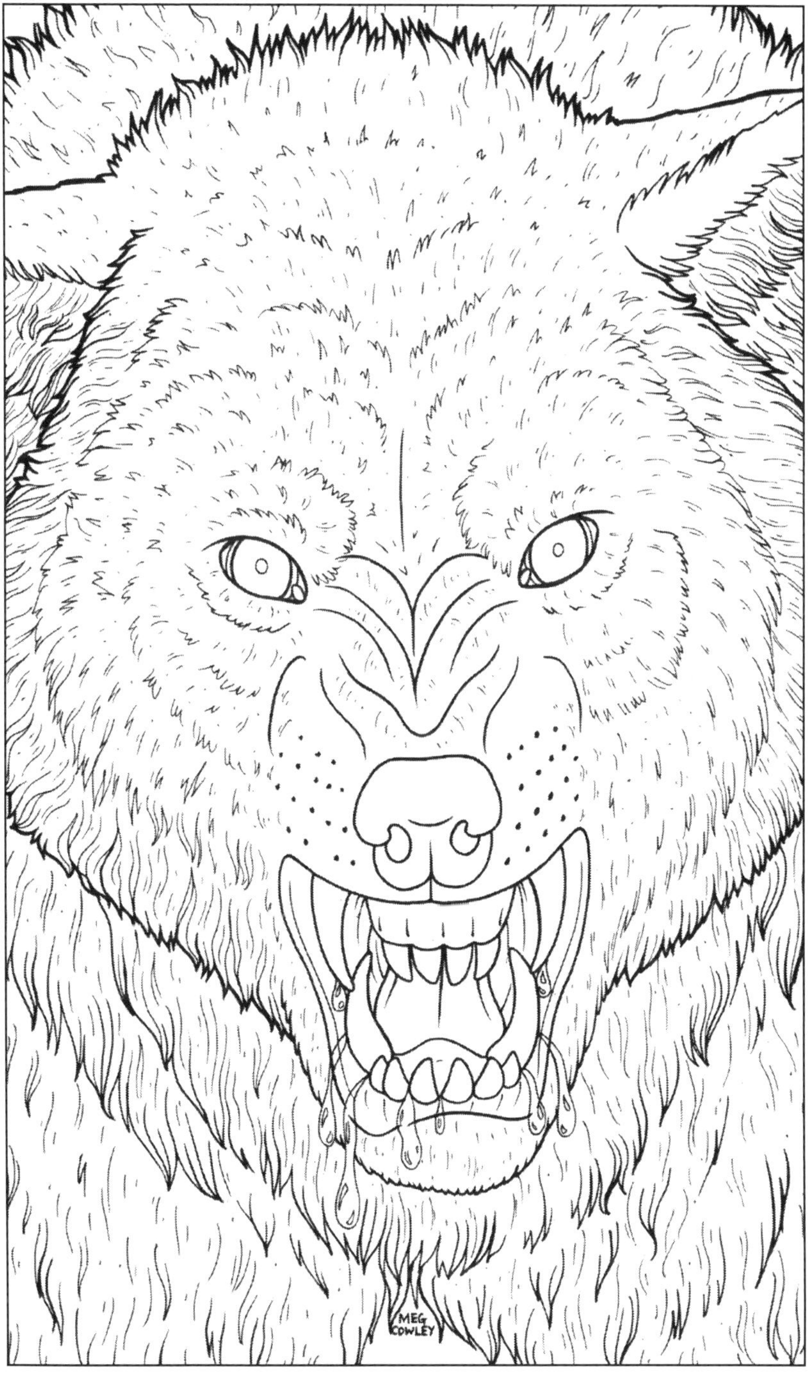
MEG
COWLEY

Grim

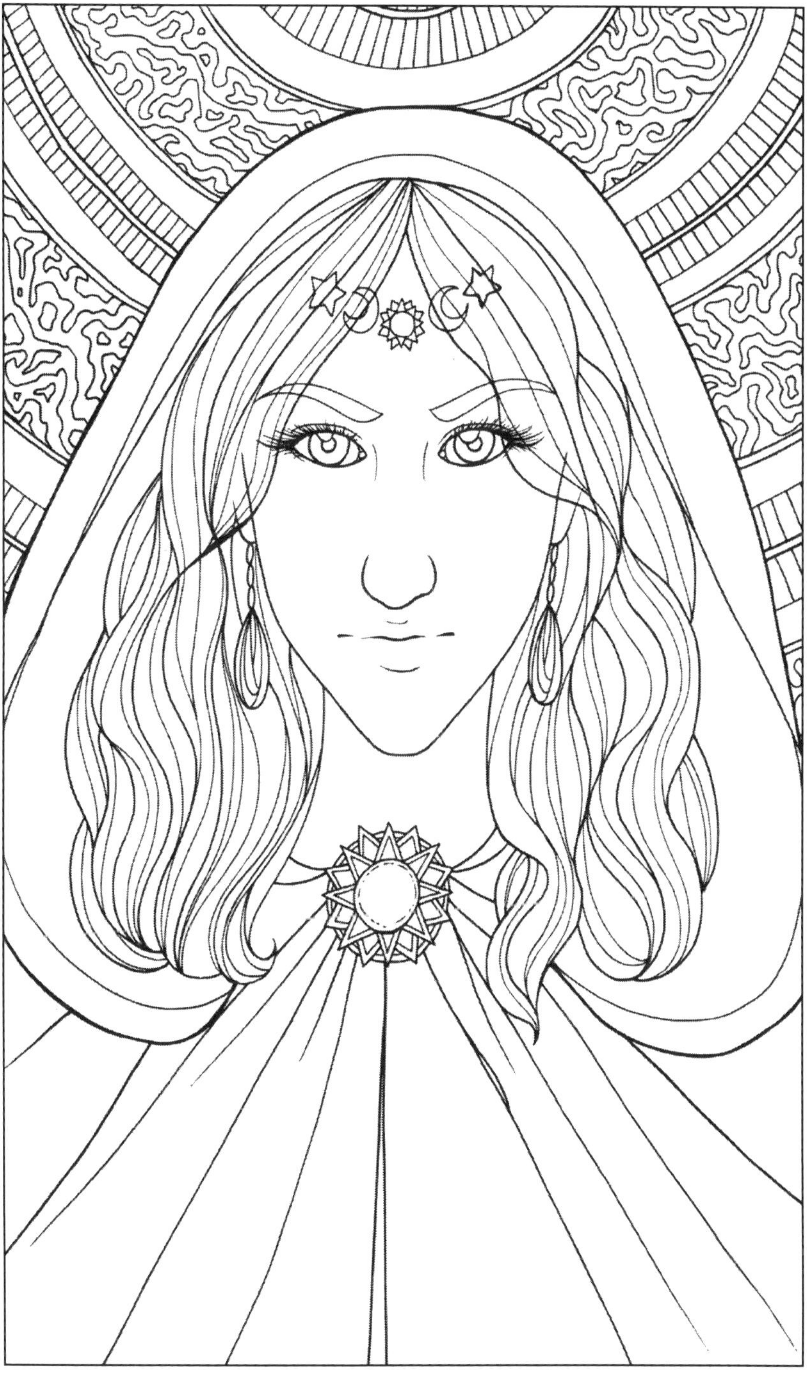

Witch

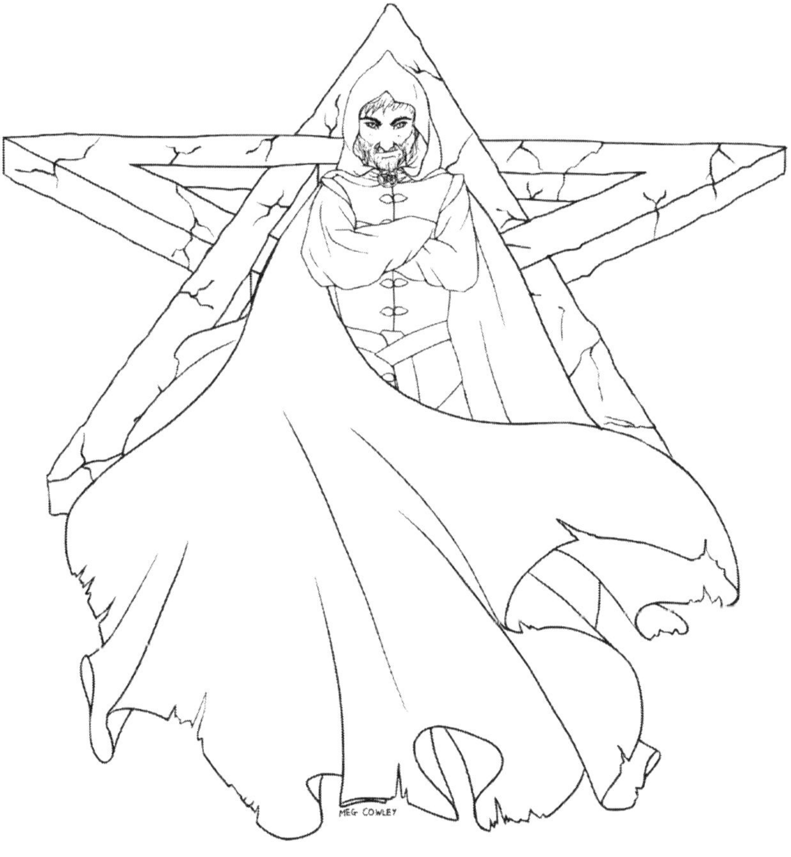
MEG COWLEY

Sorcerer

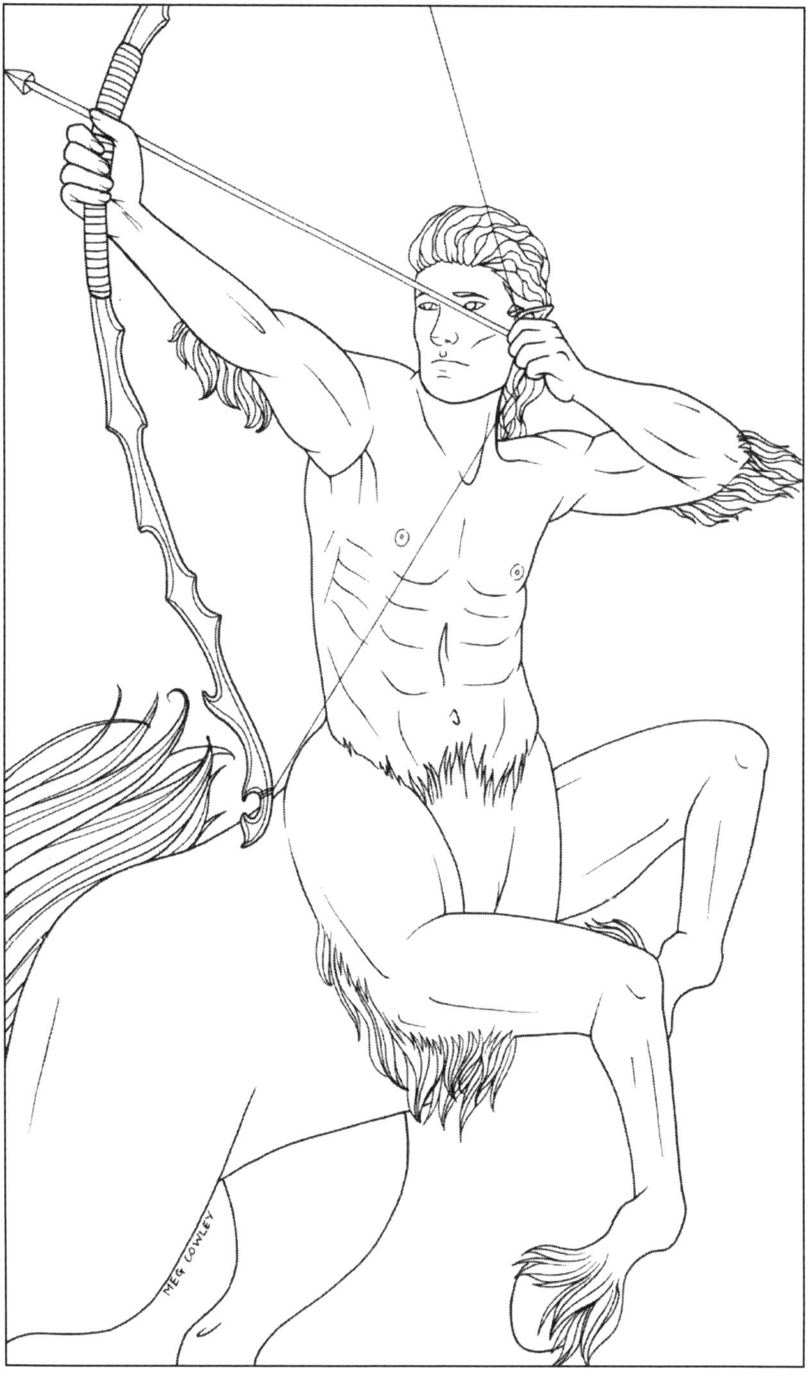
MEG COWLEY

Centaur

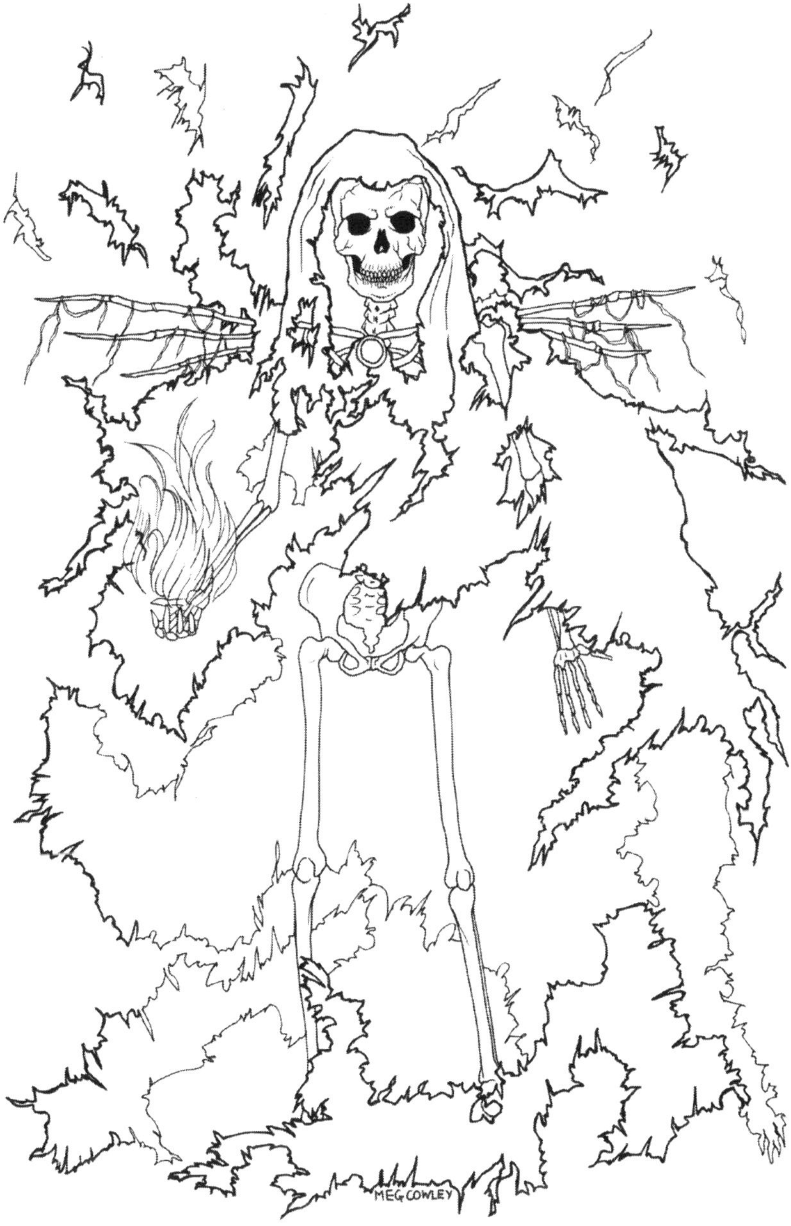
MEG COWLEY

Revenant

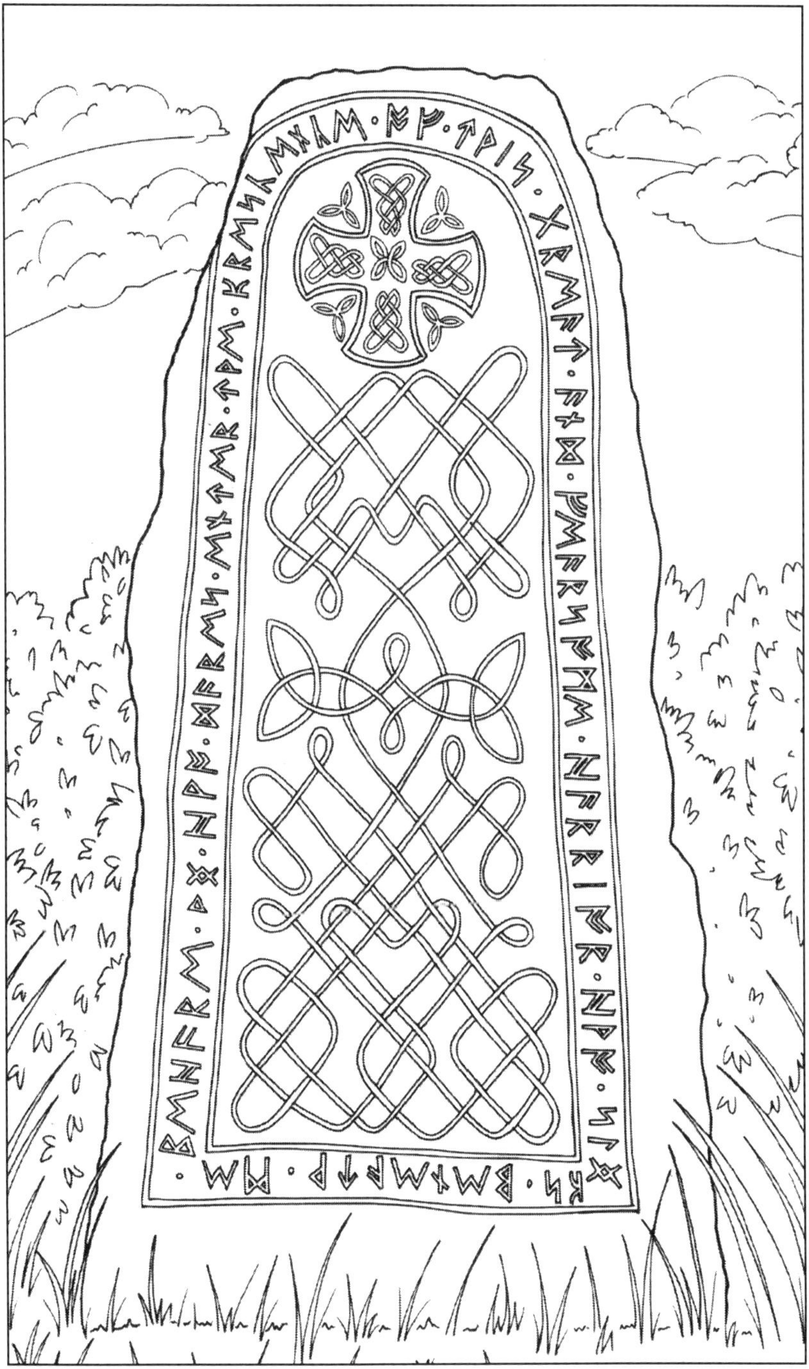

Rune Stone

Claim your free digital copy

Limited time offer!

Claim your bonus PDF download of the Fantasy Creatures Colouring Book today to enjoy even more colouring! Print your own unlimited amount of copies of your favourite pages for your personal enjoyment*. Visit the address below, enter your email address and your book will be delivered to your inbox.

www.megcowley.com/fantasybonusbook/

Sharing, resale, and distribution of the PDF download is not permitted and is a breach of copyright. All rights reserved. This is a bonus gift for purchasers of the Fantasy Creatures Colouring Book or Pocket Colouring Book in paperback.

Thanks for colouring

If you enjoyed the Fantasy Creatures Pocket Colouring Book, I would really appreciate a rating and review on Amazon to help other colourists find and enjoy it too!

Feel free to share your finished designs with me – I love to see them! You can send them to me at: meg@megcowley.com, via Twitter (@meg_cowley), Instagram (@meg_cowley) and Facebook (facebook.com/megcowley).

The Exotic Colouring Book

Free Colouring Pages

If you want even more goodies to colour, sign up to my colouring newsletter at:

illustration.megcowley.com

You'll receive exclusive free colouring pages each month, chances to win my new books, behind the scenes info about my work and more!

About the illustrator

Meg is an author and illustrator living in Yorkshire, England, with her partner and their two cats.

Meg is inspired by nature, great works of art and fiction, and her writer & artist friends around the world. She likes to experiment and try new ideas and usually works best when fuelled by earl grey tea and margherita pizza.

Meg has completed a variety of private commissions and her own design projects over the past decade, mainly digital fantasy/semi-realism paintings and graphic design projects related to her writing.

In her spare time, when not writing, reading, or drawing, she enjoys recurve archery, hiking, sleeping, gardening and cooking.

Visit **www.megcowley.com** for more information.

Printed in Great Britain
by Amazon